STRONG WOMEN CRY TOO

by

Linda Fenton

Acknowledgements

Writing this book has been a wonderful but also challenging journey. I really don't think I would have completed it if it were not for Alex Maxwell.

Alex encouraged me to tell my story and try not to cover up the truth when it came to my mental health and how I fell into the black hole of depression. Without him this story would be a censored version of my life, and I would still be covering up the immense pain that I have endured.

Our many conversations about life have been frank and honest, and we are both on the same wavelength when it comes to how important our one life is.

On top of that he is a great yoga teacher.

Thank you, Alex.

I would also like to acknowledge Claire McGregor of Kookaburra Hill Publishing Services. Dealing with Claire was a pleasure and her professionalism with editing my book was a wonderful experience.

Thank you, Claire.

To the son I adore.

Love you to the moon and back.

Contents

Preface

When I started thinking about writing this book, many years ago, I wrote a note and put it into my purse that simply said, 'Write a book'. I wanted to write about my unfair dismissal case and about all the horrible things that had happened to me in the workplace; not just the sexual harassment but also the bullying. I wasn't brave or strong enough at the time for fear of being harassed and bullied even more. But I won't be silent anymore. It is bloody well not okay.

We might have laws in place to 'protect' people against these types of behaviours but, unfortunately, many still don't come forward. It's hard, really hard, to come forward and go through a process that will undermine you and make you out to be a bad person. The company I worked for tried to do that while I was going through my unfair dismissal case.

In the years that followed, the events that happened in my life – from losing more jobs, being made redundant and the breakdown of my marriage – spiralled me into a black hole of depression.

Turning my life around from rock bottom was the hardest thing I've ever done, but I hope that writing this book will help others with depression and anxiety so they can recognise that hiding it is not going to make it go away.

As much as writing has been cathartic, it has also made me more passionate about not just improving my mental health but also to hopefully encourage more women to speak up and be heard. To stop accepting bad behaviour from men when it comes to sexual harassment but also the continued discrimination women have to deal with in the workplace and in society in general.

Chapter 1

Workplace wars

I have had many battles when it comes to the workplace because of discrimination, bullying and sexual harassment. Over the past forty years I have worked for numerous businesses in permanent, casual and temporary positions. Due to this I have observed how many organisations fall short when it comes to dealing with workplace culture. I have seen great people who worked hard lose their jobs and watched bullies get away with treating people poorly. I have had to deal with being sexually harassed, and I am guilty of keeping silent. I have witnessed many people, both men and women, being bullied, predominantly by management. Discrimination comes in many forms, but for me it was because I had a baby.

Like many people, I have lost jobs because profits came before people. Every time I started a new position, I hoped that this job would be different but, sadly, I have found that companies who look after their staff are hard to find.

I have always performed my work duties, and I've never been dragged into the office and told that my performance wasn't up to scratch or that my sales were too low. In fact, when it comes to sales, I have always excelled. I have never bullied anyone, and generally I get along with most people. I have tried to stay away from those I didn't like as, let's face it, you don't like everyone you meet and that includes the workplace. If I did have to deal with people I didn't get along with, I kept it professional. I never had a meeting with someone that ended up in a shouting match, but I've most certainly heard them coming from offices behind closed doors.

The only time I recall being called into the office and having a discussion about my workplace conduct was because I was accused of having an affair with another colleague. I can categorically say I was not. Just because you have lunch occasionally with a male colleague doesn't mean you're having an affair!

When I think about the jobs I've lost, it was mainly because of hidden agendas. Even in the first job I had I was dismissed only because the company was receiving a government benefit that paid half my wages for the first year. So, after working a year with them, I was sacked, and yet I'd never been spoken to previously that I wasn't doing my job properly.

When I say the words 'workplace wars' I refer to the fact that when we are at work it can be a constant battle to keep our positions. If something inappropriate occurs, most people keep quiet because they want to keep their job. If you want to get ahead, then you really have to devise a strategy to outperform your opponents. I'm sure you've heard of the term 'climbing the corporate ladder'. Now that is where the real battles occur. In a lot of ways, corporate ladder climbing has become the modern-day battleground, predominantly for men. Women are making inroads in traditionally male-dominated positions, but the glass ceiling is still hard to crack.

When it comes to large companies and corporations, plus many small businesses as well, it is all about the bottom line: making money. I am sure many of you have worked for companies that make a lot of money but keep cutting staff. We live in a world that is continually talking about growth and productivity, which means having more people in the workforce, yet many companies want to have fewer people working for them.

Of course, companies have to make money to keep operating, but so many cut staff as a first line of defence when profits are slipping. The term 'Too many chiefs and not enough Indians' was a common statement I heard in many companies where staff cuts were primarily at the lower end of the organisational ladder and senior management positions were rarely touched. Another saying that comes to mind is 'top heavy', where a company has too many managers because they have cut staff from so many departments that they have more managers than people on the ground.

Restructures and takeovers are designed to make a company bigger and better plus increasing their share price on the stock exchange. Unfortunately, many people who work for these companies are made 'redundant' in the process and are thrown onto the scrapheap because the company needs to improve the bottom line, and reducing staff is the quickest way to do it. I have lost count of the people I have known this happen to, including me.

Back in 1996, when I was made redundant while on maternity leave, it was due to a 'restructure' of the business, and due to 'operations reasons' that my job no longer existed. I filed an unfair dismissal claim with the Industrial Relations Commission and, subsequently, I went down a gruelling path where false accusations were made against me. The company did everything in its power to discredit me.

In my case, one of the laws that was raised in the final decision was:

170DE. (1) An employer must not terminate an employee's employment unless there is a valid reason, or valid reasons, connected with the employee's capacity or conduct or based on the operational requirements of the undertaking, establishment or service.

It was stated in the decision from my court case that the company had the capacity to offer me an alternative position, but I was never given this opportunity. In reality, it would have been the same job but with more customers to look after. So, more work at the same pay.

Does that sound familiar to you?

Over the years I've heard lots of stories about people losing their jobs due to restructuring, and it seems to be happening more and more. The difference now is that law *170DE (1)* no longer exists.

In the current *Fair Work Act 2009*[1], the state of play when it comes to redundancy is:

389 Meaning of genuine redundancy

(1) A person's dismissal was a case of genuine redundancy if:

> *(a) the person's employer no longer required the person's job to be performed by anyone because of*

---

[1] https://www.legislation.gov.au/Details/C2021C00189

As you can see, a lot has changed but sadly not for the benefit of the employee, only for the employer. Changes in laws over the years have made it easier to dismiss a person based on 'operational requirements', and the person who is dismissed hasn't a leg to stand on if they want to file for unfair dismissal.

I completely understand that if a company goes belly up, you'll no longer have a job and you won't get any redundancy payout because there is no money to give you. In some cases, there are genuine reasons for cutting staff because the company is not doing well, and they have no other options. But from what I've seen, if a company isn't doing well and needs to cut staff, they will dismiss the ones who have worked with them for less than a year. All employees who have worked for a company for less than twelve months cannot file for unfair dismissal, regardless of the situation.

People who have worked with a company for many years, and who are willing to take a redundancy payout, are not offered it because the company has to pay them too much. Some of these people have lost interest in their job and need to move on, while newcomers who are enthusiastic and want to make a valuable contribution to a business are made redundant because it's cheaper and easier to let them go. Decisions are made by management on the cheapest way to cut staff instead of looking at who is not performing well or who the best people to keep are that will help improve company profits.

Companies take over others, restructure and move to other areas; things change, and some jobs change too. So, a company can do all of these things and get rid of people they don't want working for the organisation anymore and use changes in 'operational requirements' as the reason for dismissal. Of course, the company has to comply with obligations regarding redundancy payouts, depending on the number of years you have worked for them. But within months of making someone redundant, there is nothing to stop the company employing a new person under a different position title, such as from a Customer Service Manager to a Client Coordinator, or Marketing Manager to Marketing Director. It is just a change of name, while the position is fundamentally the same.

Unfortunately, a lot of companies use a restructure as an excuse to cut staffing levels or to get rid of people who are not deemed 'team players'. I have seen many occasions where managers dismissed people just because they didn't like them or because they considered them a threat to their own positions.

The following is an example of a case that went through the Fair Work Commission[2] where redundancy was used as an excuse to make permanent positions into casual positions:

Four applicants contended that their terminations, as full-time permanent employees, were not genuine redundancies and as a result they believed they had been unfairly dismissed. The

---

[2]

https://www.fwc.gov.au/documents/documents/benchbookresources/unfairdis missals/unfair-dismissals-benchbook.pdf *applicants were initially employed as casual employees in July 2012. They were all appointed to full-time permanent positions in August 2012. On 19 February 2014 the respondent wrote to 43 employees, including each of the applicants, notifying them of their redundancy and advising that their employment would come to an end on 20 March 2014. The respondent offered each applicant employment as a casual employee. This offer of casual employment was not taken up by any of the applicants. The respondent also provided the applicants with a list of available positions at an associated entity. None of the applicants expressed any interest in the available positions. The Commission was satisfied that the respondent no longer required the applicants' jobs to be performed by anyone due to changes in the operational requirements of the respondent's enterprise following a direction from its client. The Commission found that the fact that casual opportunities remained did not detract from the need for the respondent to reduce the full-time permanent workforce. The Commission was satisfied that the consultation requirements set out in s.389(1)(b) of the Fair Work Act had been met, and that it was not reasonable in all the circumstances for the applicants to be redeployed within the respondent's enterprise or an associated entity. The Commission was satisfied that the applicants' redundancies were genuine redundancies. The Commission held that on this basis the applications cannot succeed and must be dismissed.*

Now in this case, which I might add is actually a real case but I have left out the company's name, they gave casual employees full-time permanent positions, then two years later made them redundant but offered them their casual positions back. They filed a case of unfair dismissal fundamentally because they were offered their jobs back, but only on a casual basis.

It seems clear in this case that these positions were not casual at all. They were employed as casuals, then made permanent, and then offered their casual work back, which was clearly not casual work.

Many companies hire 'casual' workers, and it is such a loose term when it comes to work:[3]

A casual employee does not have a firm commitment in advance from an employer about how long they will be employed for, or the days (or hours) they will work. A casual employee also does not commit to all work an employer might offer. Casual workers have no guaranteed hours of work, usually work irregular hours, don't get paid sick or annual leave and employment can end without notice.

Having worked in numerous 'casual' positions, I know for a fact it is abused. I worked for a large organisation that considered me 'casual', even though I was given a fortnightly roster that stated the hours I would be working each week on a regular, ongoing basis. Many of the staff at this organisation were 'casual' and they had worked there for many years on an ongoing, regular basis, but were never offered permanent work, even though it was permanent. If you couldn't work for whatever reason and informed the manager, you were crucified for letting the team down. But if the company didn't require you to work, they only needed to give you two hours' notice.

The reason a lot of companies put you on as a 'casual' is because they can sack you whenever they want to with no repercussions.

---

[3] https://www.fairwork.gov.au/starting-employment/types-of-employees/casual-employees

You can be a loyal employee but, God forbid, you ask to be put on as a permanent employee with all the benefits.

Under the Fair Work Act[4] version implemented on 22nd April 2021, some changes were made in regard to casual employment only because so many casual employees lost their jobs due to the COVID-19 pandemic. None of them were entitled to either JobKeeper or JobSeeker payments from the government. Subsequently, many casuals continued to work and spread the virus.

The new definition of casual really hasn't changed much at all:

A casual employee who has worked for an employer for at least 12 months and has, during at least the last 6 months of that time, worked a regular pattern of hours on an ongoing basis may be entitled to be offered, or request, conversion to full-time employment or part-time employment.

An employee can approach the employer and have what is called a 'casual conversation', which is the terminology used by the Fair Work Ombudsman. In this 'casual conversation' it is determined whether you are entitled to be employed as a permanent employee. The employer has to make an offer to you in writing, and you have to respond within twenty-one days after making the assessment. If you think this sounds a bit confusing, then reading the full meaning of 'casual' will probably do your head in.

---

[4] https://www.legislation.gov.au/Details/C2021C00189

I would also like to point out that small businesses with fewer than fifteen people do not have to offer you a 'casual conversation' at all.

The reality of having a 'casual conversation' with your employer about being employed as a permanent because you meet the requirements will most likely be the cause of your dismissal. As a casual, you can be terminated from your job with only a couple of hours' notice. The employer can dismiss you and just put on another casual, and then the new person has to be employed for twelve months before they can be eligible to have a 'casual conversation' about their employment.

If the government thinks that having a 'casual conversation' with your employer will make it easier to be employed as a permanent, they are delusional.

Frankly, it's a rort.

From the early 1980s to the mid-1990s, casual employees in Australia grew from around 13 percent to 24 percent. The most recent statistics from 2016 show that 25 percent of employees around Australia are casual. My guess would be that this has increased again by 2021 and will continue to grow.

How can it be that 25 percent of our working population is 'casual' in the true definition of the Fair Work Act? I estimate that it is about 5 percent, and the other 20 percent should really be employed as permanent workers. The sad reality is that if a 'casual' pushes to become permanent, and even speaks to the human resources/pay person about the hours they're working and that they constitute being employed permanently, chances are they will lose their job.

No doubt many believe that it's best just to stay silent and keep their job.

On that note, I would also like to refer to 'Human Resources' (HR). In my experience, HR departments rarely accomplish much when it comes to protecting people. They really have no power to actually stop someone from being dismissed. They ultimately take direction from senior management when it comes to terminations. You can make a complaint to HR about someone who has bullied you or sexually harassed you, but they will just follow procedures and try to resolve the situation so it is seen to be dealt with. Even if it is proven that a staff member has done something wrong, it comes back to management to make the call to dismiss an employee. When I first started working, there wasn't a HR department at all, and if you wanted to complain about something or someone, you had to go to your manager. This was not always a good thing, particularly if it was your manager you wanted to complain about!

Before the term 'Human Resources' was created, it was fundamentally a section of a company that dealt with payroll and employment arrangements. Now, it deals with many more facets of a company including hiring of employees, training, performance issues and, of course, issues of discrimination, bullying and sexual harassment within the organisation. It has changed considerably over the years as this department also ensures the business has all the policies and procedures in place so that everyone knows their rights and how to make formal complaints about procedures and unwarranted behaviour by other staff members. But they still can't make the final decision to dismiss an employee.

I have to say that I've had little to do with HR departments, other than being provided information on my position and having someone from HR sit in on a job interview. I have never used them to make a complaint about anyone, and if I did have a procedural issue, I usually spoke to my direct manager about it. The reality is that these departments don't really have much influence when it comes to making a complaint as they are usually overseen by a senior manager, who will sweep a lot of complaints under the carpet and do little to help the person who is being bullied or had sexual advances made towards them. In the situations where I was sexually harassed, it was usually a manager that did it. Yes, not only did I get dismissed from jobs, but I also endured sexual harassment and bullying. All of these things contributed greatly to my downward spiral into the black hole.

The Human Rights Commission inquiry of 2020[5] states:

... most people who experience sexual harassment never report it. They fear the impact that complaining will have on their reputation, career prospects and relationships within their community or industry. Through the inquiry, the commission heard of the need to shift from the current reactive, complaints-based approach, to one which requires positive actions from employers and a focus on prevention.

I agree that this needs to happen because the current systems in place in most workplaces simply do not work. With the case of Brittany Higgins that emerged in 2021, it's not working in

---

[5] https://humanrights.gov.au/our-work/sex-discrimination/publications/respectwork-sexual-harassment-national-inquiry-report-2020#fn1

Parliament House either, the very place where they implement our workplace laws.

When it comes to HR, I believe this should be an external division of any business, so that they can investigate complaints without being influenced by managers within the organisation. If a person feels comfortable that they can make a complaint without thinking it will fall on deaf ears or fear losing their job, then more complaints will be made, and this will positively impact workplace culture. I also think the processes should be swift and not prolonged, so that the person accused is dealt with and moved on or transferred to another department or dismissed due to unacceptable behaviour. If the person making the complaint has made false accusations, then they must also be dealt with in a similar way.

I am not naive in thinking that every complaint is warranted, but through personal experience, and seeing many despicable things happen in the workplace, it is usually the perpetrator who gets away with it and the victim who leaves the company.

Brittany Higgins was influenced to not make a formal complaint to the police about her rape at Parliament House because she was concerned about losing her job. It was swept under the carpet because the Liberal Party didn't want to lose face in an upcoming election. Her mental health was obviously impacted by keeping the 'secret', but two years later she couldn't continue to be quiet about what had happened to her. She was very brave to come forward.

She was taking on the big boys in parliament and that must have been a scary prospect. I took on a large corporation with my unfair dismissal case and I was also up against a male-dominated organisation, and I can categorically say that it was very scary.

If the leaders of our country in Parliament House can't get their act together, then how can we possibly expect every company in Australia to do the right thing?

I am well aware that you can make complaints to the Human Rights Commission[6] about bad behaviour within an organisation, but usually the complaint is made after the person has left the company. The process of complaints is a drawn-out one that causes stress on the person making the complaint. Many complaints take over 12 months to be dealt with, which is the same amount of time it took for my case to go to court.

When it comes to these timeframes, I understand that information needs to be gathered, but the fact is that many people just don't have the time or the energy to go through this process. It would be interesting to know how many people have made a complaint to their HR department and nothing was done. In my experience, companies will go to great lengths to cover up what they have done. The companies I worked for had no regard for me as an individual, and they were only concerned with covering their own arses.

Let me put it into perspective.

When I filed for unfair dismissal, the company I worked for spent thousands of dollars on a legal team to refute my claim rather than admit they had done the wrong thing.

---

[6] https://humanrights.gov.au/complaints#main-content

Just think what could have happened if they had admitted fault when I lodged my claim. I would have gone back to the job I loved and continued my career. I knew I was an asset to the company but, as far as I know, many of the male managers didn't think I was management material. I know, without a doubt, I would have made a great manager. The company would have benefited from having a female perspective in a male-dominated environment, and I would have ensured that the culture changed for the better. I was respected by my customers for providing excellent service and, at the end of the day, a business is not a business without its customers.

Most organisations will have policies and procedures in place regarding bullying, harassment and discrimination, but, in my experience, they were just words on pieces of paper (or should I say a computer). I have seen these so-called policies at many companies, but I have also rarely seen them followed. The only reason they seem to be in place is so they can show they have them, and that is all.

When you interview for a job, you will often get an information pack about the company and what is required from the position. They will usually have the organisational policies for you to read as well. They will make out that the company respects all its workers, and they have all the best practices in place but, in reality, they could just be words with no action.

The company I worked for at the time I fell into the black hole of depression had all the policies and procedures in place to try to deal with bullying, sexual harassment and discrimination, and they were attached to my employment contract. But, without a doubt, this company was totally incompetent when it came to dealing with the bullying I experienced. I had to deal with bullying from one of the salespeople, the operations manager and the transport manager.

The salesperson I worked with was rude when he spoke to me and made me feel like I was an idiot. He constantly harassed me about his orders being processed in the computer, even though he gave me most of them with incorrect information in the first place. He just expected everyone to clean up his mess. Because I was new to the company it gave him the opportunity to blame me if something went wrong, but the fact was that he stuffed up lots of orders before I even started working there.

The operations manager would just walk away from me and ignored me when I asked him questions. It was obvious to me that he simply didn't want to work with me. The questions I asked were about orders for clients, who wanted to know what was going on. Companies won't exist without their customers, but clearly the manager had forgotten this was the case. He just saw me as interfering in his job when all I wanted was an idea of when customers would receive their orders and therefore be able to advise them of this.

The transport manager had a lot of pull in the company and, frankly, most people feared her. She was extremely reluctant to help with any type of training or information to assist me with my job. She knew the salesperson was harassing me, but she just sat by and let it happen.

I told my immediate boss what was happening, but both of us were new to the company and still finding our way. He had seen that it was a difficult and complex company to work for with a lot of unworkable procedures. He said he would get me help but, unfortunately, that never came. I spoke to the managing director at the time, and at this stage I broke down in tears. He was sympathetic and knew I wasn't getting the help I needed to do my job. He said he would help, but once again nothing happened.

One day, while talking to the occupational health and safety person, we spoke about what was going on in the company and also about her challenges while working there. She knew I was being given a hard time by other employees, but in her position she could do little except be someone I could talk to.

When you look at this company's website, they state that they value their employees and full training is provided – not unlike many organisations – but it's not until you actually work for a company that you find out if they actually do.

Chapter 17 is about my experience at this company and the impact it had on me. It's called *The final straw*, and I go into more detail about what happened and what followed.

When it comes to sexual harassment, I have endured my fair share, but I was not raped. Brittany Higgins admitted that she decided to come forward about her situation because of the Australian of the Year 2021, Grace Tame,[7] who is an advocate for survivors of sexual assault. Grace was raped by her teacher while at high school and couldn't talk about it because laws existed to prevent assault survivors from talking about their experiences, and therefore protecting the man that raped her. She fought for many years to have the laws changed so she could tell her story and subsequently became Australian of the Year 2021. What a woman.

---

[7] https://www.australianoftheyear.org.au/recipients/grace-tame/2297/

In 2018, the then prime minister, Malcom Turnbull, introduced a 'bonk ban',[8] where ministers, regardless of whether they were married or single, could not engage in sexual relations with their staff. Doing so would constitute a breach of the standards. This was introduced because the then deputy prime minister, Barnaby Joyce, was having an affair with a younger staffer who later became pregnant with his child. Joyce had consistently denied any involvement with the staffer. He was also front and centre when it came to being against same-sex marriage and called himself a 'family man' who was devoted to his wife and children.

In 2020, a *Four Corners* investigation, called 'Inside the Canberra Bubble'[9] reported on Minister Alan Tudge allegedly having an affair with staffer Rachelle Miller and the toxic culture of Canberra. Miller lost her job because of this relationship while Tudge remained in his position, regardless of the fact he was clearly in breach of the bonk ban.

The bravery of these women bringing forth their stories encourages other women to come forward. This gives me hope that women are sick and tired of being abused and used by those in positions of power in the workplace.

This bravery inspired me to write this book and tell my story of discrimination, bullying and sexual harassment. Most of my situations occurred when I was young, particularly the sexual harassment, but it is obvious to me that little has changed over the years.

---

[8] https://www.afr.com/politics/federal/anthony-albanese-imposes-labor-bonk-ban-20201111-p56dls
[9] https://www.abc.net.au/4corners/inside-the-canberra-bubble/12864676

A toxic, male-dominated workplace culture hit the news on 21st June 2021, when the CEO of Sony Australia, Denis Handlin, was removed from his position by the US parent company after an investigation by *The Guardian*[10] into longstanding complaints by female employees of bullying, harassment and discrimination from top-level executives. There were cases of women, either pregnant or on maternity leave, being made 'redundant' from the company and having to sign non-disclosure agreements (NDAs) so they could receive their redundancy payments. Due to the NDAs, they could not file for unfair dismissal and therefore this protected the company from any legal action.

It is what I refer to as 'shut-up money'.

In a *Four Corners* investigation that aired on 11th October 2021, called 'Facing the Music'[11], former employees exposed the toxic culture of Sony. The systemic bullying and sexual harassment by the CEO went on for forty years and complaints were swept under the carpet. The people who did complain were paid shut-up money and signed NDAs so the incidents were never raised again. Some of the former employees that were interviewed in the program said the company was ruled by fear and intimidation and most employees kept silent due to concern of losing their jobs. Many of them still struggled with what had occurred to them and that Sony Music did not address this behaviour and allowed it to continue.

This is a large organisation with a HR department that reported to the New York head office about the ongoing issues, which

---

[10] https://www.theguardian.com/culture/2021/jun/21/sony-music-australia-allegations-toxic-work-culture
[11] https://www.abc.net.au/4corners/facing-the-music:-the-sony-music-scandal/13579828

either did nothing or had their hands tied when it came to dealing with complaints.

When watching this program, it felt like I was hearing about my personal story from twenty-five years ago, but this was in the headlines in 2021. Cases like this show that workplaces are beginning to be held accountable, but there is no doubt a long way to go. Companies can't continue to push these issues aside by paying employees shut-up money and having them sign NDAs so the complaints go away.

For women who fell pregnant while working at Sony, it was well known that they would not return to their position and would ultimately be made redundant.

The Respect@Work: Sexual Harassment National Inquiry Report (2020) by the Human Rights Commission[12] sets out the issues to try to deal with sexual harassment in the workplace. It states:

Workplace sexual harassment is prevalent and pervasive: it occurs in every industry, in every location and at every level, in Australian workplaces. Australians, across the country, are suffering the financial, social, emotional, physical and psychological harm associated with sexual harassment. This is particularly so for women.

... Through the Inquiry, the Commission heard about the way in which power disparities in society, as well as in the workplace, enabled sexual harassment. Overwhelmingly, the Commission

---

[12] https://humanrights.gov.au/our-work/sex-discrimination/publications/respectwork-sexual-harassment-national-inquiry-report-2020

heard that gender inequality was the key power disparity that drives sexual harassment. Gender inequality relates to the unequal distribution of power, resources and opportunity between men and women in society, due to prevailing societal norms and structures.

When it comes to proving that someone raped you, having to go to court and talk about it again and again would be unbearable. I get why a lot of women don't want to bring charges against someone because the toll it takes on you is enormous. I think men are well aware of this and that is why this type of behaviour continues to get swept under the carpet.

Even though the Human Rights Commission wrote the Respect@work report, it seems to me that it will sadly be a long time before anything improves while men are the ones who have the majority of power, not just in business but also in politics.

Chapter 2

Workplace harassment

When I think of how many times I was sexually harassed at work, it was a lot. Many of the incidents were things I brushed off as a bit of a joke. I will admit that I think political correctness has gone a bit overboard over the years, and if you can't have a bit of banter then life becomes boring. I guess the juggle on whether it is 'appropriate' can sometimes be borderline. I consider myself an open-minded person so I guess lots of men got away with saying inappropriate comments that they knew I wouldn't take offence at.

When it comes to the workplace, I've learnt that you have to be careful with what you say or do. In reality, your work colleagues are not your friends, they are colleagues you work with in a profession or business. Yes, you might have times when social events occur or you meet up at the local pub after work on a Friday night, but you still have to be careful. Getting drunk with colleagues can be the most dangerous thing you can do when it comes to sexual harassment. Sadly, many women find this out the hard way.

The first time I found myself in this situation I was about twenty. I was working for a large financial firm that threw around money like there was an endless supply of it. Leading up to Christmas our department and a few other sections had a separate, impromptu night out. We went to a local restaurant and then later to a bar to 'kick on'. I have to say that many drank too much, but when the company pays for everything most people will take advantage of it.

As the night went on, I was dancing with some of the other girls in my department when, all of a sudden, a senior manager put his arms around me and started grinding himself against me. At first, I just went along with it until he really started to get hot and heavy with me. Luckily for me the song that was playing at the time changed and it gave me the opportunity to say I needed to get a drink and take a break from the dancefloor. He insisted I stay for another dance, but I managed to do a runner.

When I got back to my table, the other girls were all asking me what the hell was going on. I was shocked as this manager would have been twice my age, plus he was married. He made a few more moves on me that night, but I ended up leaving before I got into a situation I might not have been able to handle. It's a situation many women have had to deal with and make the decision to leave out of fear of what might happen.

When it comes to Christmas parties, we all have a story. That is why many companies now don't provide alcohol at events or it's limited so that it's more civilised. It's a smart move really because when lots of alcohol is supplied you can bet someone will abuse it and inappropriate behaviour is more likely to happen. Back in the 1980s, this type of behaviour was something you just accepted. Unfortunately, this still happens today but at least there are more procedures in place to try to deal with it. I'm sure many situations still go unreported as it is usually the victim who endures bullying because they have made a complaint.

I worked for this company for about eighteen months and finally left as I disliked working in the city. Catching the train to work every day was a pain, so I applied for another job working for a large snack-food company. Something different to finance too, as working with numbers all day had become boring and monotonous. I wanted to be more involved in sales and marketing, dealing with customers directly and not just always sitting at a desk. The new position involved promoting new products to the company's client base, and I was part of a team that had to travel a lot around Victoria and Tasmania.

With this company, once again, I worked with a lot of men in the sales department. On one occasion I was standing in the doorway of the sales manager's office and, while talking to him, I could see that his eyes were looking at something behind me, and he was clearly distracted. All of a sudden, I could feel someone close behind me breathing down my neck. 'Your place or mine,' said the person to me in a very sexual manner. It was the general manager of the company.

He had done this to me before in the tearoom while I was making coffee but, on this occasion, it was in front of the sales manager and other members of the sales team (all men, of course). I took a big risk and turned around and said, 'Well, my husband is away this week so we can set a date for you to come to my place.' He just looked at me in shock and the other sales members almost fell on the floor laughing so loudly that others in the building were wondering what the hell was going on. The general manager said nothing and just walked away. He was clearly embarrassed that everyone was laughing at him and, subsequently, he never came anywhere near me again. A brave move on my part.

On another occasion, while working for the same company, I was away in Tasmania with a group of salespeople as we were trying to increase sales in the area. We all gathered for dinner every night to discuss the day. One night, while walking down the hall of the hotel, I knocked on the sales manager's door and yelled out, 'Are you ready for dinner as I'm heading down to the restaurant?' He opened the door, and he was just wearing his underwear. I stood there in shock, not just because he wasn't wearing much but I was thinking, *Bloody hell, he's fat!* While he was standing there in a sexy (or trying to be) stance, I just said, 'Well, I guess you're not ready.' He said, 'Why don't you come in while I get dressed?' Naturally, I declined and said I would meet him downstairs.

At another company I worked for, a new sales manager had been appointed and the sales team were going out for dinner for a meet and greet. Once again, too much booze was on offer and, while talking to the new boss, he just came out and said, 'How would you like to have the best orgasm of your life?' Stunned to say the least, I declined politely and left to go home soon after. So, once again I was the one who left for fear of a situation getting out of hand.

At another company I worked for we were out at a sales function, and I was the only woman there out of thirty men. Two guys I worked with had become good friends and we used to hang out together. They both used to joke around with me a bit, but I could give it back and, frankly, I enjoyed joking around with them. Once again it was a sales manager that came up to me and said, 'Do you know you have the best tits I've ever seen.' The other two guys just looked on in shock, and I think they thought I would slap him in the face but, instead, I said, 'Thanks for that,' rolled my eyes and walked away.

Unfortunately, I had to work with this man, and on every occasion I walked into his office to discuss something, all he did was look at my breasts. One time, I put my head to the side and bent over slightly to catch his eyes and said, 'I'm up here,

Michael,' while pointing to my eyes. He shook his head and was embarrassed that he was caught out. He made a point of never doing it again.

On all of these occasions I never made a complaint as I knew at the time it would fall on deaf ears, and also the managers would make my life difficult at work. This was a common theme, and I don't believe it is that different today. We still have a long way to go when it comes to this type of behaviour at work. Just because you have 'policies' in place doesn't stop it from happening. Just like a lot of women who get raped in the community, they don't report it as they feel they won't be believed or that they 'asked for it' because of the way they were dressed or the fact that they were nice to some man. Just because a woman is wearing a 'sexy' dress or is speaking to a man in a friendly way doesn't mean it gives the man the right to rape them. When it comes to women, looking 'sexy' can sadly come at a huge price.

There have been many court cases over the years where a man is accused of rape and the lawyers representing him will use the fact that the woman provoked the man by the way she was dressed and that she was 'looking for it'. So many men have either not been charged or their sentence is so light that the woman walks away wondering if laying charges was even worth it. The stress of having to go through a court case and reliving what happened would be horrifying.

Being violated in such a way and then having to live with the fact the man who raped you got away with it would be so hard to deal with, but sadly many women have had exactly that. The mental scars would take a long time to heal, if ever.

Just because men are stronger than women does not give them the right to do whatever they want. Because they are physically stronger does not make them smarter either. It is bloody stupidity and ignorance that makes men think they can do this to women, and women are bloody sick of it.

It is time for men to wake up and see that women deserve better and need to be treated equally.

Men and women have to come together and resolve this issue; it is not just for women to solve. It starts with fathers and mentors educating boys from birth and role-modelling respectful and appropriate ways to interact with women. The media needs to change its language around victims of sexual assault and how cases are reported on, and women need to be heard and listened to when allegations are made. We can't do it on our own, and more women have to be in management positions, have seats on boards and hold positions in politics for this issue to stop.

Discrimination is another issue that comes in many forms and is still a major issue around the world. My court case was all about discrimination as I was discriminated against because I had a baby. Whether you are female, male, non-binary, transgender, gay, straight, black, white, young or old, equality is something we all must strive for.

Back in the 1980s, little was done about bullying, discrimination or sexual harassment. The *Racial Discrimination Act 1975* was the first major anti-discrimination legislation passed in Australia, aimed at prohibiting discrimination based on race, ethnicity or national origin. It is interesting to think discrimination laws in Australia started in the 1970s, some fifty years ago, but as much as we have seen some improvements with protests, such as Black

Lives Matter and the MeToo movement, there is still so much more needed to change our society. Men and women have to come together and stop this kind of behaviour, and all of us will benefit from a much happier society.

They say that times are changing and when you look through history much has changed, but we still have a long, long way to go before true equality exists.

Chapter 3

My childhood

Have you ever thought about your very first memory? Looking back to your childhood and remembering the first thing that comes to mind is not as easy as you'd think. I am sure most people can remember something from a young age; mine was when I was four.

I recall being taken to kindergarten for the first time by my mother. When I got to the entrance I held onto both sides of the gate and started screaming that I didn't want to go. Mum had to pry my hands off to get me inside. It would have been quite a scene, yelling and screaming that I didn't want to go. My recollection of me standing at the gates is still vivid today, and I find it interesting as to why this image is my first childhood memory.

Frankly, I think it was a sign that I was a determined young girl with a strong will, and I was not ready to go.

Born on 20th March 1964, I was the 'baby' in the family, being the last child with two older siblings. My brother was the eldest and then my sister; we all had a couple of years between us. My sister and I shared a bedroom at a young age, and when it came to having our own space, it was a contentious issue. I recall one time when my sister put white sticky tape down the centre of the room, along the floor, up the set of drawers and even the mirror! When my father saw it he went ballistic and ripped the tape off, but it left a permanent mark so the 'your side' 'my side' remained forever. When my brother was about fifteen my parents let him stay in the family caravan in the backyard, so my sister and I could have our own rooms. I was so glad to have my own room as I was the tidy one.

My parents were both born in Australia. My mother was one of four girls, and my father was one of twelve. I have great memories of having lots of cousins to play with at family gatherings. On my mother's side it was the end of the family line due to having four girls. My grandfather was an only child as his father, my great grandfather, was killed on the battlegrounds in Europe during WW1, and his brother was injured in Gallipoli and died of his wounds in a hospital in Egypt, and he never had children.

My mother was the eldest. She married my father at the age of eighteen and my father was twenty-five. Within a year my brother was born. Mum didn't get any support from her mother due to her mental health condition, which was diagnosed as schizophrenia back then but today she would have been diagnosed as bipolar. My mother has told me about my grandmother's erratic behaviour and how difficult she could be. In her later years, she was on a lot of medication, and I remember her taking lots of tablets to deal with her condition. My grandfather was the sole provider who looked after his wife and provided for his family, and they lived a modest lifestyle.

My father came from a poor family. His father died when my father was only fourteen. My grandmother did it hard; she raised her children in a rundown house, and my father has told me that he often didn't have shoes to wear when he went to school. His older siblings did a lot to help out, and my uncle also helped out a lot financially with his winnings as he was a professional racehorse bookmaker. He purchased a new house for my grandmother, and over the years the whole family used to gather there for her birthday and Christmas, and I can assure you it was not a quiet affair with lots of laughter. I know without a shadow of doubt that my talkative and loud voice comes from my father's side.

When I started primary school at the age of five, I was one of the youngest in the class; other children could be up to eleven months older than me, which is a big gap developmentally at such a young age. Nowadays, many parents keep their child back when starting school as this gives them a better advantage. I wish I'd started school a year later as my education could have turned out very differently.

I always felt less intelligent than the other kids, but I was fairly social and got along with most of them. Like every school there was always the bully or a leader of the gang. Whether it be boys or girls, someone became the leader of the pack, and that was certainly not me.

I do remember one incident where a bully told all the other children to not play with me all day. I had to stay on my own while some teased me, and others were too scared to say anything for fear of being banished like me. This bully, who was in fact a girl, used to pick different girls to banish on a regular basis. I actually became friends with her, certainly not to bully others but as the saying goes, 'Keep your friends close but your enemies closer'. I stayed friends with this girl for many years, and when I look back I can see it was really for the same reasons, and that was to keep the peace and it was safer to stay friends.

When I got older this friendship was just hard work and I hated the way she treated people, so I decided to finally walk away. I really wish I'd walked away earlier as this person constantly crushed my confidence and it took many years to gain that back. I never really caught up in my primary school years, and when it came to going to high school that is when it became obvious that I was well and truly behind.

I hated high school most of the time. I did have some subjects I liked but they were cooking, art, needlecraft and pottery. I absolutely hated math, and it never helped that I had a math teacher for a number of years that everyone hated. He used to deliberately drop his chalk on the floor and then, while bending down, he would look across under the desks and see if he could get a glimpse of some frilly knickers that the girls might be wearing. It was the joke of the school as he did it in every class. I am sure the other teachers knew, but nothing was done about it.

My first year at high school was a nightmare. I remember getting my first report and it was a disaster. I failed three subjects: English, mathematics and history; the rest I scraped through.

I remember dragging my old reports out from what my son calls 'my treasure chest', which is a wooden chest given to me by my grandparents when I was around twenty. This chest contains so much: photos, birthday and wedding cards, my reports and my diaries. Even when I was looking at my old reports the shame of how poorly I did in subjects like math and English came flooding back like a tidal wave. Many memories of school came back; something I'd pushed to the bottom of the barrel a long time ago. Looking at these reports and reading the comments by teachers showed I was clearly struggling.

Many teachers wrote that I was talkative, and people that know me now would not be surprised by the revelation that I am. But I find it interesting that I wasn't considered talkative as a young child while in primary school; it was only when I got to high school that this became an issue. I think that engaging with the other students in the class was more interesting than what the teacher was talking about. I was not a naughty child, and when I was told to be quiet, I did what I was told.

When it came to English and reading, I rarely read any books. As a young child I hated reading and only did it for school assignments. The first book I actually enjoyed was *1984* by George Orwell. The book focused on the consequences of totalitarianism, mass surveillance and repressive control of people's behaviours within society. I found it fascinating. We had to read it for social studies, and I enjoyed talking about it in class. Many thought it was a stupid book, but for some reason I loved it. At the time I read it, back in 1978 (I was only fourteen), it was only six years until it would be 1984. So much of the book seemed like fantasy, but I also wondered if the world would actually end up that way in the future. Would we be under constant surveillance and controlled by corrupt governments?

How horrible that would be!

Now, when I look at what the world is like today, it feels like much of what I read back then *is* actually happening.

Both my junior and senior school years were at government public schools and getting extra help was something that just didn't happen. The senior school I went to had a bad reputation but it was the closest to our house, so that is where my sister and I went. My brother went to a local technical school for boys only. Technical schools taught subjects like building, plumbing and electrical trades, and girls were not allowed to go. The unfortunate thing about that is I would've probably performed better at a technical school than a mainstream school, but I was a girl and there was no choice. My brother ended up becoming a plumber by trade and found a job as soon as he left school. My sister was not an 'A' student but she definitely did a lot better than me. She ended up going to college and became a geography and biology teacher.

Me, I just plodded along. I could have put more effort in, but I always felt that I was just dumb and putting more effort in was just a waste of time. I did put work into the subjects I liked, which involved creativity, but they were subjects you never considered as a career as they involved the arts.

In my final year at school, when I was sixteen, I managed to pass all the subjects but one: English. I remember being put in a class that was full of the 'smart' students and thinking, *What the hell am I doing in this class?* I tried to get a transfer to another class, but it didn't happen. Maybe I was put there to give me a push along.

This is what my English teacher wrote in my final report at the end of the year:

Linda has been a pleasant and co-operative student who has participated well in class discussion and she acquitted herself well in the oral examination. Unfortunately, however, Linda's written work is not up to the standard of her verbal ability and she had difficulty with 5th form written work, mainly because she hadn't mastered the fundamental skills of written expression in the early years, an absolute essential for a demanding 5th form year. In spite of this, Linda demonstrated some very good personal qualities such as perseverance and determination and was always conscientious and is to be commended for this.

Sadly, I still failed.

I needed to pass English to be able to do Form 6, which was the final year (HSC) at school, and this enabled you to go to college.

When saying my goodbyes at the end of the year, a number of my teachers said they were surprised I wasn't going on to do my final year. Most students didn't back in the day; about 80 percent didn't, in fact, and it was only for the kids that wanted to go to college. I had thought about doing my final year as I would be away from the other students who distracted me, and maybe I would do well. But failing English put a stop to that. Some of my other teachers thought it was horrible that my English teacher had failed me, and I was offered a complimentary pass by the school so I could do my final year. Sadly, I didn't take up the offer and it is still something I regret today. Failing English just confirmed to me that I was dumb and wouldn't be able to complete my final year at school.

It's interesting to think that I always knew I was behind and needed a bit of extra help, and my final report for English actually states that I hadn't mastered fundamental skills of expression in my early years. Well, tell me something I don't know! Unfortunately, back when I was a young girl, I always just thought I was dumb.

Encouragement was something I rarely received. Many parents nowadays seem more focused on their children's school efforts. My parents worked full-time and didn't really have the time to help me with schoolwork, and tutors were not in abundance like they are today.

From a young age I recall being left to my own devices as my parents would go away for the weekends in the caravan on their own. As a teenager at the time, I didn't really want to go with them anyway and preferred to hang out with my friends. The first time they went away without me I was only fourteen. My brother and sister were meant to look after me, but as soon as the caravan turned the corner at the bottom of the street, they could not get out of the house quick enough.

So, for most of the weekend I was on my own. I did have a couple of friends come around and we drank some of my parents' alcohol. We didn't really need much to get drunk, so my parents didn't miss anything, but it was the first time I got intoxicated. I could have told my parents that my brother and sister left the house and didn't look after me but the ramifications would not have been worth it. As much as I know my brother and sister would have been given a good tongue-lashing from my parents, but it would have been worse for me as I would've endured a bigger backlash from my older siblings. Best that I just kept quiet.

I remember one time when my parents went away and word got out at a local pub that my house was an 'open house'. This meant that a party was going on and anyone could come. Thank God mobile phones were not around then as I would've had hundreds turn up. I remember taxi after taxi rolling up and within an hour or so the back family room was packed with people. Most of them I knew, and they were aware that my parents were away for the weekend. Some I didn't know but there was no trouble, and, in fact, it was a bloody good party. I was lucky it didn't get out of hand.

The look on my sister's face when she got home and saw a party going on was not a happy one. I was at the bar in the corner of the room as a friend and I were making sure people couldn't steal my parents' alcohol. She came up and started screaming at me about having a party while Mum and Dad were away, but I remember saying, 'Well, if you (and my brother) didn't piss off as soon as Mum and Dad left, this wouldn't have happened.' She couldn't deny that was the case so she just joined in.

When it comes to siblings there are always some issues. It could be rivalry, jealousy, feeling inferior and even hatred. I don't hate my siblings at all, but we've definitely had our issues over the years. When it came to feeling inferior, I most certainly felt that. My brother and sister used to tell me that I was adopted, and because there was no formal baby photo taken of me, I used to believe it. My brother and sister had professional baby photos taken of them when they were around ten months old, but there was never one of me. I don't know why one wasn't taken, but I guess by the time I came along life had gotten busier and maybe my parents didn't have the money. Not having a baby photo is really not important now that I'm older, but the thought that I might actually be adopted stayed with me.

When I was about fifteen, I recall a family friend saying that I looked like my dad. I remember not feeling that great about it at first, as being a girl and looking like your father wasn't really a compliment as far as I was concerned. Later in life I could see the resemblance. Over the years I've been told that I look like my father, and other times people have said I look like my mother. On many occasions my sister and I were told we looked alike, so over the years the thought that I might be adopted faded. Unfortunately, as a child it upset me greatly. At the time my brother and sister were just teasing but it does prove that when cruel things are said to you, they can stick and impact your self-worth for a long time.

Like in many families back then, the boy was number one, and our family was no different. My brother was good at football, and during the football season going to the local oval and watching him play plus helping out with canteen duties or taking the oranges out at half-time was a weekly duty. My parents were heavily involved in the football club and that consumed a lot of their time on weekends.

My sister and I didn't play any sport, but we were all taken for swimming lessons from a young age. The main reason for the swimming lessons was that we used to go camping most school holidays and it was usually somewhere near the beach. I'm grateful that I got to learn to swim as it was something a lot of children in the area didn't do.

When it came to doing other sports, I did a little bit of netball with some girls that lived down the road when they needed a fill-in, but that was the extent of my sporting career. I was never encouraged to do it; not that different to most girls my age back in the '70s. Even when it comes to women's sports today it's considered second-rate by many. When women started playing football a lot of men thought it was ridiculous they were playing a 'man's' sport. In every sport around the world where both men and women play, sadly women still get paid much less than their male counterparts.

More women have sporting careers now and young girls have more female role-models they can look up to, but it wasn't something I had when I was growing up. I wasn't aware of any female role-models on anything back in the '70s. I am sure some women were doing great things, but you never heard about it. Even now, when you google famous women of the '70s, it's mainly models and actresses who come up. Yes, I did love

Charlie's Angels with the three female detectives kicking arse, but I don't recall what you would refer to as 'professional women' in the public eye.

Girls just grew up, got married and had babies, and, if you were lucky, you might become a model or an actress.

Chapter 4

Being in the adult world

When I left school in 1980, I was still only sixteen and, like most teenagers, I thought I was grown up and knew everything there was to know. I had finished my school years, but the one thing school doesn't prepare you for is the adult world.

Before I started looking for a job, I went on a camping holiday with my family to Port Macquarie on the New South Wales coast. It was the last big camping trip I had with my parents. I have fond memories of the holidays we had over the years but this one would be my introduction into the adult world.

Even though I was only sixteen, I looked older, therefore I never got asked my age when going out to hotels or nightclubs. On this holiday my parents were okay with the fact I was going to the local pub. There was little else for someone my age to do. My sister, her friend, my cousin and I would go out and have a few drinks at the local pubs, and it wasn't long before we started talking to the men there. On a couple of occasions, we would be walked back to the caravan park and maybe end up on the beach for a bit of a pash with these young men, but it never went any further for me as I was still a virgin. I wasn't about to have sex with some man I'd just met.

When it came to sex, I obviously knew what sexual intercourse was, as I was told all about it at high school, but that was the clinical version. When I was about fifteen my father saw me kiss a boy at our front gate. Later that day, he pulled me aside and we had a chat in the backyard at the outdoor table and discussed 'boys'. Yes, it was my father who spoke to me about boys, kissing and, of course, sex and the real ramifications of what could happen when you go down that path.

I remember that conversation quite well as I recall being a bit shocked that my father thought I might have sex with this boy. Bloody hell, I was only fifteen. The truth was that many girls got themselves pregnant at a young age and this conversation with my father was about not getting pregnant. An aunt of mine had fallen pregnant at a young age and he saw how that impacted her life, and he didn't want that to happen to me. We spoke about going on the contraceptive pill and that maybe it was something I should consider. I assured him I wasn't ready to go down that path (and I really wasn't) but he said that girls have to be careful as being with a boy can get out of hand, and before you know it you could be doing the deed, have no protection and fall pregnant.

He said, 'Boys are not the ones who have the baby, you do, and you'll be the one looking after the baby when the boy doesn't want to have anything to do with you anymore.'

I recall one girl at high school who got pregnant; she was whisked away and it was rarely spoken about. You also had the girls that had a 'reputation' for having sex with boys, but that's something that hasn't changed even today. When a boy has sex with lots of girls, of course, he is a legend, but the girl is just a slut.

On this holiday I was about to learn the cold hard facts that when you show a man some interest, he automatically thinks he's going to have sex with you. As much as I'd kissed a few boys by the time I was sixteen, this holiday threw me into the male world; not boys but men.

I met a man at the pub we frequented; he was a local to the area and we had spoken on a couple of occasions while down at the beach. He was much older than me, around twenty-five, if not older. He was your typical surfer type with long curly hair, great body and lots of charm, very easy to fall for. I remember bumping into him down at the local shops and, as we walked along the street, he held my hand and gave me a kiss on the cheek when I had to leave. *Wow*, I thought, *what a catch!* I couldn't believe that someone like him would be interested in me. I always thought I was a bit ugly and fat, but now I can look back at photos of me when I was young and I was not that at all. I actually had a great figure but, like most females, I had my body issues and was influenced by beautiful models on the front of magazines.

One night when we were all at the pub, I told my sister that I was just going for a quick ride with this man back to his house so he could pick something up. I was not so naive to think that nothing would happen, and I hoped that I would get to have a good pash, but what eventuated was far more than what I was prepared for.

We did drive back to his house, I stayed in the car and he ran into the house and picked up a bag; it was a small bag of marijuana. I wasn't shocked as I'd seen dope before and knew some people who'd smoked it, but it wasn't something I'd ever had. He asked me to put it in my bag, which I was reluctant to do but did it anyway. As we drove off, I thought we were going back to the pub, but he went off in a different direction. I asked him where we were going, and he said we were going to a lookout near the beach. It was dark so there wasn't going to be much to look at, and that is when I knew I was in trouble.

We ended up at a secluded area in a carpark that was empty. As soon as the car stopped, he was all over me. We kissed passionately and I hoped that this was all he wanted, but of course it wasn't. It started to get more heated, and that is when I said I needed to get back to the pub as my sister would be worried, but this didn't concern him at all. He was trying to get my clothes off and that is when I started to really panic. I told him I didn't want to do this, but he persisted. When I finally told him I was a virgin he just looked at me in shock. I remember feeling embarrassed about it, which is silly as a lot of girls were still virgins at sixteen. When I told him how old I was, he backed off a little. As I'd met him at the pub, he'd assumed I was over eighteen and that I wasn't a virgin, and because I had showed some interest, he naturally assumed that I wanted to have sex with him. Why men 'assume' you want to have sex is beyond me, but the sad reality is that the large majority do.

As we were at a place where I had no idea how to get home, it was dark and somewhere out of town, the thought of doing a runner scared me, and I thought he would just chase me. He persisted in fondling me and forced his hand down my pants. I didn't fight him off as I thought that if I didn't let him do something, he'd get angry and do more harm. I kept telling him that I really needed to get back as my parents would be getting worried, so he stopped and dropped me back. When I got back to the caravan my sister and her friend were already there and starting to panic about where I was. I didn't tell them what really happened as I was embarrassed. I felt like this stupid girl who'd got in over her head. The next morning, I realised I still had the bag of dope in my handbag.

When I showed my sister and her friend, they said we should keep it, but I was shitting myself. We were going to be returning to Melbourne in a couple of days and I didn't like the prospect of having my parents find me with a bag of dope. That night at the pub I saw the man and gave it back to him. Why, I don't know; I should have dumped it. He showed no interest in me that night, which I was glad about as I wasn't interested in having a repeat performance either. He thanked me and went on his way, clearly knowing I wasn't prepared to give him what he wanted.

When I think back on this, and the fact that I came so close to being raped and how scared I was, I'm also lucky this man didn't persist that I have sex with him, as I wasn't on the pill and he clearly didn't have condoms, so I could have easily ended up pregnant. The very thing my father had spoken to me about and how things can get out of hand, and ultimately out of my control when it came to men having their way. Many fathers would not have this conversation with their daughters, but they should. When it came to talking about sex, it was often the mother who spoke to their daughters and the father to their sons, so teenagers may have only got a one-sided view of things. Thankfully, I think this is changing now.

The discussion I had with my father stayed with me, and I was a lot more cautious after my horrible experience while on that family holiday. Sadly, though, this was not going to be the last time a man thought he could have his way with me. I have been subject to a lot of sexual harassment over the years, and I had to learn how to deal with it.

For the next year after that holiday, I partied with friends, drank too much, kissed a few more boys; yes, they were just boys as most were the same age as me, and then I fell for one of them who later became my husband, and he was the first man I ever slept with. He was a respectful person, and he would have never pressured me into sex.

My husband and I dated for about five years, got engaged and then married on 6th December 1986. We met through mutual friends and were just good mates for the first year, but it grew into a full-on relationship.

Our wedding happened on a boiling 38-degree day, and I recall sweating in my wedding dress. While we were in the middle of the ceremony, I saw a bead of sweat running down the side of my husband's face while he stood there in his suit. It was the usual stock-standard wedding of the '80s and we had about one hundred guests. We were married in a Catholic church because my husband was raised in a Catholic family. Even though I was christened in the Church of England, my family was not religious at all, but I went along with the Catholic ceremony even though I would have preferred to get married on a beach.

I did what he and his family wanted because of their religion. If I was to do it all over again, I would never get married in a church, but I was young and ultimately pressured into it. I did get my way when it came to not having a full Catholic service that would have gone on for over an hour, and we just had the wedding ceremony instead. Lucky, really, because it was a bloody hot day. The day after the wedding we went on our honeymoon to Queensland at my uncle's holiday house on the Gold Coast.

We did the usual things young married couples do and purchased a house and took on the inaugural mortgage. Our house was in the outer suburbs of Melbourne; a standard three-bedroom home with a big backyard. We both worked full-time and contributed to the finances and saved money on the side to travel.

The first ten years of our marriage we travelled a lot, did the traditional Bali holiday and then went to Thailand as well. In between we also took various holidays around Australia. Our last big trip before I got pregnant was a seven-week holiday to India, England, Scotland, Belgium, Amsterdam and Egypt.

After our holiday we sold our house in the outer suburbs and moved into, what you would call, a renovator's delight. It was a 1920s weatherboard home that we lived in for over twenty years and I worked hard to bring this home back to life.

I wasn't interested in having children until I hit thirty, and then I thought, *I better get a move on with this as I'm not getting any younger*. At the time I had a great job that I was doing well at and, in reality, I put off having a child as I wanted to continue my career. At the age of thirty-two, I had been working for this company for almost seven years when I had my beautiful baby boy.

I was only twenty-two when I got married – too young really – but in some ways that is how I thought it was meant to be. My brother was twenty-one when he got married and my sister was twenty-three, so I just followed suit. Even back in the '80s most people got married before they lived together, unlike today where people try before they buy. Frankly, I think that is a great idea as you really get to know someone when you live with them. If I had my time over again, I wouldn't have married at such a young age.

I love how most young people today travel and party more before they settle down. You need to do that as it's part of finding yourself and learning more about life and the different people you meet along the way. You see friends come and go, you stick with the people who're likeminded and let go of the ones who go down other paths, as the sad fact of life is that not all people are your people.

When I look back and remember my twenties, I had a lot of fun, but people change, and so did I. I see myself as such a different person then to who I am now and how the real world is, how cruel people can be and the impact they can have on your life. There are good people out there, but I have found that there seems to be more people in the world who have such a disregard for other people's feelings, they are so consumed with their own life and having the biggest house, the fastest car and making lots of money is their only focus. These people lose sight of what truly matters in life.

Millionaire Malcolm Forbes said, 'He who dies with the most toys wins,' but I have also heard it said, 'He who dies with the most toys dies anyway.' Steve Jobs, founder of Apple, stated on his deathbed: 'At this moment, lying on the bed, sick and remembering all my life, I realize that all my recognition and wealth that I took so much pride in, have paled and become meaningless in the face of impending death.' He was one of the wealthiest men in the world, but money was nothing to him when he was dying.

The saying, 'You can't take it with you when you die' is something I've said on a lot of occasions, and it's a fact; you can't. Money is nothing when you are sick and dying. Of course, we need money to live and put a roof over our heads and food on the table, but when it all boils down to it, having great wealth doesn't buy you happiness; another great quote.

The workplace can be cruel and unforgiving, where some people think they can treat you like crap and not have a second thought about it. When you start a job and meet new people and, in the workplace, socialise with them more, you may think some of these people are your friends but, in reality, they might stab you in the back if they think it will benefit their career or cover up a mistake they've made. Cynical, yes, but it's been my experience and I know that many other people have experienced the same thing.

Climbing the corporate ladder and making more money than anyone else is so important to some people and they will do anything to achieve their goals. When they are at the top of the ladder, they forget about the people at the bottom who are actually the ones who keep the business operating, but sadly they are treated like a number. When an organisation needs to cut costs, I have seen, on more occasions than I can remember, that it is the bottom rung that gets chopped first.

Another saying I love is the one I mentioned earlier: 'Too many chiefs and not enough Indians'. It is so true for many companies: too many people giving orders and not enough people to carry them out. Top-heavy businesses where the men at the top look after their mates on big fat pay packets while the people doing the hard work are on minimum wage.

I thought you could progress in a job if you did it well, but in thirty-five years of working, I found out the hard way that this could not be further from the truth, especially if you are a woman.

Chapter 5

My first job

Back in the '70s girls weren't really told we could do anything we wanted. It was different for the boys as they could be a doctor or go into law, always much higher-achieving jobs than what the girls were told about. I remember being in class one day and the teacher asked us what we wanted to do when we left school and went to work. Most girls said they wanted to be a hairdresser or a secretary. A lot of the boys said either a builder or some type of trade. As I lived in a working-class suburb, not having lawyers or doctors as parents meant that we didn't think we could go down this path, and from what I recall many were not encouraged to become high achievers.

When I left school in 1980, I was sixteen. I was unemployed for about three months after the end of Year 11. I was on unemployment benefits and applied for a lot of positions and it felt like I would never get a job. Like 90 percent of the other female students, I was out there looking for a junior position in an office environment. I was good at typing while at school, so an office job seemed to be the best road to take.

It seemed like I was always just missing out when suddenly I was offered two positions at the same time. One was for a law firm in the city in administration, and the other was a travel company that did bus camping tours around Australia. It was walking distance from home and, as much as I was interested in the position in the law company, I really didn't think I was smart enough, and I was even surprised I'd been offered the job. I had always underestimated myself and I guess that's why I took the job at the bus company.

I was the junior clerk, and I did all the mundane things that other people didn't want to do, but that was fine as I was happy to learn the ropes. I knew you had to start somewhere. I worked hard and didn't complain about some of the extremely boring jobs I had to do. I got along with everyone and was keen to learn more about the travel industry. I remember the first job I did, ruling lines in a blank-paged book and thinking, *Why didn't they buy a book that already had lines in it?* They were available in all news agencies! I said nothing and continued to do that all day. As the week progressed, I did the usual junior work: filing, making coffee, doing the mail, going to the bank. I did find it interesting that they'd send a seventeen-year-old girl down the street to the bank with a mixture of cash and cheques in a cloth bank bag, which made it obvious I was going to the bank. I did it anyway.

On one occasion when I was going to the bank, I just did my usual walk up the street, taking my time as it was a nice sunny day. On my return to the office, I could see some of the staff looking out the window. I just waved and thought, *Shit, I must have taken too long.* I walked up the stairs thinking I was going to get blasted, but one of the ladies in the office came up and gave me a big hug and said, 'Thank God you're back.' Everyone seemed relieved to see me and I thought, *What the hell is going on here?* It had just been on the radio that a girl in the area had been kidnapped and people were currently trying to find her. She was taken just across the road from where our office was and the description of her was a bit similar to me, so the office staff had all been in a panic thinking it was me that had been taken.

Later that night, the girl's body was found; she'd been murdered. They did find the man that did it and it seemed to be just a random violent act. I considered myself lucky that it hadn't been me. Even after that I still had to take the money to the bank every day, even though it was really something one of the men should have done. Rather than just walking down with a bag of cash, someone could have driven and parked at the back of the bank and been a bit more careful about the process. But that wasn't even given a thought.

While working for this company, I was sent on a trip to far north Queensland to see how the tours operated and obviously learn more about the company. I was overjoyed that everything was paid for (other than my own personal expenses) and that I would be going for about ten days. I flew into Cairns, which had a small airport at the time. I sat waiting for the bus to pick me up. I waited and waited and waited. After about four hours I thought, *Something is very wrong here*, and wondered what I should do. It would have been a simple exercise today with mobile phones, but we're talking about 1980. I went to the customer service desk and asked if they knew anything about a bus coming to pick me up, but they knew nothing. They were helpful in letting me use the phone to call the office in Melbourne to find out what was going on. The office organised for a taxi to come and pick me up. By then I had been at a hot airport for six hours. It was dark when the taxi picked me up, and the airport was just about to close for the night. Being only seventeen at the time, I was scared as I had no idea where I was going and hoped that the taxi driver was going to take me to the correct place.

I arrived at the caravan park where the tour group were staying, and the bus driver, cook and courier – the people doing the tour –

had no idea they were supposed to pick me up; they were never told by the office I was even coming. They felt very sorry that I had spent six hours at the airport not knowing what the hell was going on. I had some dinner from the camp kitchen and headed for my tent to sleep as I was exhausted.

The next day, all the people on the tour had a free day in town to look around and do whatever they liked. There was a mixture of Aussies, Canadians, Americans and Germans on the tour, and they were all young, but I was the youngest. We all got along well, and even though I came into the tour about a third of the way through, I fitted in.

I remember spending most of the day at the large waterslide that was about five stories high and in the centre of town. A lot of the other women wouldn't go on it, but you couldn't stop me. Waterparks were just starting to open up in Queensland, so this was a new experience for everyone. They had four slides of various speeds. I went on the first one and then straight to the fastest one; it was so much fun. The men thought I was brave going on the fast one as I was the only girl to go on it. Even the guy who was working at the slide, making sure everyone was being safe, was surprised I went on it again and again. I had no fear and had the biggest grin when going down and crashing into the water at the end; it was a hoot.

The next day we went on a day trip to Port Douglas and a crocodile park. Not everyone wanted to go, and some decided to have a quiet day. As all the people on the tour were young, a lot of drinking and partying went on, so some just wanted a rest day. About half of the people went, and I remember getting on the bus and thinking it was great that I didn't have to sit next to anyone on the bus and have to talk. It gave me the opportunity to have a nap before we got to our destination. We drove to Port Douglas first and stopped at the local pub. Back then, Port Douglas was a small country town that only had a couple of shops, a pub (of course, we were in Queensland) and a post office. It's very different today with about five pubs, many resorts and a main street full of restaurants and shops. It's a popular holiday spot.

When we got off the bus most of us just went to the pub for a drink. After a few beers the driver called for us to return so we could go to the crocodile park. Most of us went to the toilet first before returning to the bus. When I walked out of the pub, the bus had left. Usually, the courier would do a head count and realise they had left someone behind and return to pick them up. But not this day!

After about an hour and a half, when I finally realised the bus wasn't going to return, I went to the post office to use the phone. Due to the fact I had fallen asleep on the bus on the way to Port Douglas, I had no idea how far it was back to Cairns. Only wearing my sarong and bathers, I must have been an interesting sight going into the post office.

I told the man what had happened and that I needed to contact the caravan park I was staying in, to let them know where I was. He suggested I look in the phone book and search for caravan parks listed and see if one of the names sparked my memory on where I was staying. There were about ten parks, and I had no idea. While in the post office another man heard my predicament and said he could take me out to the main road, and I could hitchhike back to Cairns. I wasn't thrilled about the idea of hitch hiking, but I really had no choice. There were no taxis in the area or a public bus service. The plan was to get back to Cairns, go to the post office there and call the parks, and that way it would only be ten minutes or so for them to come and pick me up.

The man took me down to the main road, but he was going the other direction from Cairns, so he dropped me off telling me that someone would be along soon who could take me to Cairns. I started walking along the road, and it was bloody hot. I had no hat or sunscreen, and I thought I was going to bake out there. I walked for about an hour and nobody came along, and I was starting to think this was a really bad idea. All of a sudden, I heard a car coming. It was a ute with three guys sitting abreast in the front seat. They were tradesmen heading back to Cairns having finished work for the day. They pulled over, and I said I needed to get to Cairns. They said, 'Fine, we're heading there, jump in.' I was going to jump into the back of the ute, but then two of them jumped out and said, 'Sit in the front, we'll sit in the back of the ute.' I wasn't happy about this as I was more than fine being in the back and just getting a lift back to Cairns.

While driving along, the driver asked me what the hell I was doing out here and I told him my story. He was a bit shocked that I'd been left behind and said they obviously weren't a very good travel company to leave someone behind. So true! Not only had I been forgotten about at the airport, but I had also been left behind on a day trip.

We continued the drive when all of a sudden the driver pulled over and jumped out of the car. He started yelling at the other guys in the back. Thoughts were going through my mind that I was a goner. I was on a quiet road back to Cairns with three guys. My heart was beating out of my chest, and I thought these men were going to rape me and dump my body somewhere and it would never be found. I don't know why I didn't just run for it; I froze I guess. The next thing, the driver jumps back in and throws a joint (yes, marijuana) into my lap. He said, 'Those bastards were going to hog it all. Thought we'd better get our share.' I did smoke cigarettes so I thought that if I was going to be raped and killed then I might as well be off my face. I lit the joint and we continued our drive to Cairns.

Further down the road, he asked if I wanted to have a swim. I said, 'Sure, why not!' By this time, I was pretty stoned, and it was hot. I had my bathers on so I thought I might as well. We turned off onto a side road and soon arrived at a beautiful rock pool. Other people were there, so I felt safe that they weren't dragging me into the bush to rape me. The water was crystal clear, and we jumped in and cooled off. By this time, I realised these guys were fine. They were happy to help a damsel in distress. We then headed back to Cairns. I was a lucky girl.

As I had no idea where the caravan park was, the guys said they'd take me to the post office. The driver said he just needed to drop one of the guys off first then we would head into town. Driving along, still feeling pretty stoned, I yelled out, 'There's the caravan park!' I could see the bus and all the tents set up in a row. I could not believe my luck. The guys were rapt that I'd found it. We drove into the park and everyone was sitting around having a few drinks when I jumped out of the car and yelled, 'Hi guys, I'm back.' I gave the guys in the ute a hug and thanked them for saving me and for the lovely and joyful afternoon. Everyone at the camp watched in astonishment. Some came running up saying, 'What the hell happened to you, we had no idea where you were?'

The bus driver, courier and the cook were all in the bus talking about what the hell they were going to do; they'd bloody lost someone. As they didn't see my spectacular arrival, I jumped onto the bus then stated, 'You guys bloody left me behind in Port Douglas.' They asked me how I got back as they were just about to head off and return to all the places they'd stopped during the day. Obviously, they were relieved I had returned but you could see the terror in their eyes about what they'd done. They were responsible for the people on the tour and ensuring their safety, and they had stuffed up big time.

When I returned to the office after the holiday, I had to write a report on how it had gone and what I'd experienced on the tour. Naturally, I told the truth. I had been forgotten at the airport and then left behind in Port Douglas and had hitchhiked back to Cairns, but I also did say that, overall, it was a fun trip. None of the managers spoke to me about what had happened on the tour, which I thought was a bit strange. They were lucky it was a staff member that had been left behind and not a paying customer. I'm sure that if this had happened to a paying customer, they would have given them a refund.

For the next few weeks, I just did my normal tasks at work. Then one day I was called into the accountant's office, and he informed me that they were letting me go. On the day I was sacked I was completely shocked; I had no idea this was coming. I hadn't been told anything about what I'd done wrong; I was just told that I wasn't wanted anymore and that was it. As I walked out of the accountant's office, other staff members came up to me and said how sorry they were for me. They obviously knew I was going to be dismissed, and they all seemed upset by it. I was just in shock. As I walked down the stairs, it finally hit me, and I just burst into tears. I had one staff member run down after me and ask if I was okay. Well, of course, I wasn't okay. I turned around and said, 'You can all get fucked.' I was so angry that everyone knew what was going to happen to me and nobody had said a thing. I continued to run out of the office and walked home in tears.

Later that night I got more and more wound up. I ended up calling the general manager the next day and asking him the real reason why I'd been sacked. He fumbled for words and then said the report I'd made on the training tour to Queensland was very harsh and that it looked like I didn't want to work for the company. I told him that all I did was tell the truth. For God's sake, I was left behind and had to hitchhike back to Cairns and nobody had a clue where I was. Anything could have happened to me. I said I considered it lucky for the company that it was me left behind and not one of the paying customers. He really didn't know what to say, and I just knew there was more to it.

I found out later from a staff member that the only reason I was sacked was because the company was no longer getting benefits from Centrelink to pay half my wage. I was employed through a Centrelink government program that offered companies half of your salary for the first year of employment. My year was up, so they got rid of me. It had nothing to do with the report I'd made about the tour or my ability to do the job, it was all about saving money.

The company employed a new girl within weeks of me leaving, and they got the same deal from the government where they paid half her wage. The job only paid $80 a week (we are talking about the 1980s and it was a low-paying junior position) so the company saved themselves just less than $2,000 in the twelve-month period. Pathetic really.

They did not give a damn about how this would impact a young girl in her first job; they didn't give a shit. I felt ashamed and embarrassed about losing my first job, and it only made my self-confidence shrink even more. When I did find out the truth behind my termination, it did make me feel better, but the damage had been done when it came to my self-worth.

About six months later, I found out that the girl they'd hired after me was adjusting the bank slips and taking money from the bag when going to the bank. It took a couple of months for the accountant to realise this was happening. When doing a bank reconciliation with statements, they didn't add up, and only then did they realise she was taking the cash almost every day. I would never have done something like that, but I was over the moon that it was the universe telling them they had done the wrong thing by me. About five years later they went under and the company was shut down. Karma.

For the next eight years, I worked for a lot of different companies, mainly in office administration and customer service roles. Some were temporary and contract jobs and a couple were permanent, but I left those jobs because of either being bullied or being sexually harassed.

It was not until 1989 that I started my job with a large packaging company. I stayed in this job for seven years until I went on maternity leave at the age of thirty-two.

Chapter 6

My position at Amcor

I began my employment at Amcor in March 1989. The company was called Australian Paper Mills at the time but a couple of years later the name changed to Amcor Fibre Packaging and was under the Amcor Ltd banner.

The job was based at their Scoresby manufacturing facility and the position was as an internal customer service clerk. I was allocated three sales executives, who worked out on the road seeing customers face to face, while I looked after their customer base and ensured all their packaging requirements were met. At the time there were two main players in Australia for paper-based packaging: Amcor and Visy.

The customer service team comprised of five other women, all doing the same tasks. The external sales executives were all males and we all got along well. I have fond memories of my time at the Scoresby branch and the added bonus was that I was only a five-minute drive from home.

Approximately eighteen months after I joined the company, Amcor purchased a smaller packaging company in Box Hill and, subsequently, the entire sales team was moved to the Box Hill offices. It was a stressful time as it affected customers, and we had many times where orders were not being fulfilled as the systems that were in place were all changing. The domino effect of clients not receiving their packaging on time caused them to stop production of their own products, which obviously cost them a lot of money, so they were not happy campers. It was the customer service section that copped the brunt of the aggression from clients.

When we finally settled in at the Box Hill branch, we then had to contend with an 'us' and 'them' mentality. The staff that were retained from the company in Box Hill were resentful of all these newcomers invading their space. The conditions were cramped, and it was so noisy in the customer service area you could hardly hear the person you were talking to on the phone. Eventually, a larger area was created, and things started to settle down.

There were still lots of changes happening in the company – people leaving due to the amalgamation of the companies, some were made redundant and others were offered packages to leave. A position became available as a sales executive out in the field seeing clients face to face and also increasing sales in a designated area. As I had done this type of sales work before, I decided to apply for the position. It came down to me and another person, but I crossed the line because of my past experience being out on the road.

The area I took over was in a mess, and my predecessor had been dismissed due to poor performance as the territory was only producing approximately $1.5 million a year. I had a big job to do when it came to getting clients back on board as many of them hadn't been looked after well.

Being the first woman that my customers had to deal with face to face from Amcor also had its challenges as many were not confident a woman could understand the manufacturing processes that were in the various companies. I worked hard to turn everything around, and over the next five years I built up my sales from $1.5 million to almost $4 million a year. I gained a lucrative contract with a large dairy manufacturer worth about $1 million a year, and that contract was confirmed about two months before I went on maternity leave.

I recall when I told my manager I was going to try to pick up the dairy account and he told me flat out, 'You'll never get that account as everyone who's tried has failed.' That was like raising a red flag to a bull. It probably took me about six months to nail it, and I'll never forget my sales manager's face when I told him I'd won the account. I was pregnant when I won this account and was on maternity leave when the orders started to flow in.

I was told by a staff member that the manufacturing manager had said I wasn't given enough credit when it came to picking up the dairy account and the impact it had on keeping machines going at the Box Hill branch.

The sales team comprised two sections. One was called Major Accounts and they dealt with large companies whose contracts were multi-million-dollar companies. Most of these accounts had hard and fast contracts with prices set for anything up to two years. The section I was in consisted of territories. Each salesperson had a designated area around Victoria to look after, and most of the areas consisted of around 80–160 accounts. They were mainly made up of small to medium-sized businesses whereas the Major Accounts executives could be looking after about eight to ten companies and most were extremely demanding.

I enjoyed my job, and I loved the various aspects that the position provided. I had a wide range of different businesses to deal with, from spice importers, food suppliers to small car parts and quirky gift suppliers. I found it interesting going through manufacturing plants and seeing the end product. The manufacturing plant I worked at was also large and interesting, where you could watch rolls of paper coming in the door and pallets of packaging boxes leaving the factory to our clients.

The company had a large budget when it came to entertaining our clients. A large proportion was spent on the major accounts, but we all got the opportunity to take our clients out to either the Melbourne cricket ground to watch the football or Rod Laver Arena for the tennis or concerts. The company had private corporate boxes at both venues, and they were used extensively. They also had a dining table for eight at Flemington Racecourse, and I loved those days as I always enjoyed going to the races and having a bit of a punt. My father's family loved a punt on the horse races and I grew up knowing how to put on a bet and reading the racing form guide.

The corporate box at the MCG held sixteen people and all food and drinks were provided. They were fun days. I also loved the concerts, and I always got the 'younger' type events at Rod Laver Arena as most of the others in the sales team were much older. They were not interested in seeing 'loud bands' such as Bon Jovi, Janet Jackson and Lenny Kravitz. I also had a couple of ladies-only nights and saw Tom Jones and Michael Bolton. None of the men were interested in going to see them.

I also got to go to the Australian Open tennis tournament at Rod Laver Arena. I wasn't that interested in tennis, but I actually went to see some great players of the time, like Steffi Graf. I was also privileged to see John McEnroe's last game in Australia. By this stage, he'd lost all his aggro and he got a standing ovation when he left the arena. When it came to tennis it was just luck of the draw who you saw as you were just given a day (not the finals as they all went to senior managers), and you never knew who you were going to see.

I enjoyed taking my clients out as you got to know them better and built the relationship, and that is really what it's all about. Many companies around the world entertained their clients and this is something that still happens today to ensure you keep your customers happy.

The external sales team consisted of twenty-one people, all of them men except for me! We had three sales managers: one who looked after the Major Accounts executives, which consisted of six men, and the sales manager, who looked after the territory executives, which consisted of twelve, then we had the Victorian sales manager, who oversaw the whole department. I mustn't forget that we did have one other woman in the department, and she was the secretary to the sales managers. She was a lovely woman who was very professional in the way she conducted her work.

During my time in the sales division, I didn't always get along with my direct sales manager. I was always civil, but we didn't always agree on how to deal with various customers. Most of the time we had what I thought was a relatively good rapport. I believe that any company you work for you should have differences of opinions. If everyone thought the same way change would never happen and companies would not progress.

In late 1994, when I'd been in the job for three years, another sales position became available, and it was advertised with a much higher wage than mine. I was on around $40,000 a year and the position advertised was for $60,000 a year. I knew at the time most of the men were getting paid more than me, but I couldn't prove it and none of them were going to fess up to me what they were earning.

I approached my manager about the job advertised and the money that was being offered. I was told that to get qualified people they had to advertise at that wage. I then went on to say that I was aware that everyone else in the department was getting a higher wage than myself, and his answer was that it was because they all had more experience than me. So, after working for the company for almost four years, I was considered less experienced, even though in the past three years I had doubled my sales budget. The fact that most of these men had worked for the company longer than I had didn't mean they were better at their jobs. Also, I was looking after just as many clients as all of the other sales executives, and fundamentally I was doing the same job as anyone else in the division. So why should I get paid less?

I wasn't happy after this conversation and after being told I wouldn't be getting a pay increase, so I decided to speak to the general manager about it. He was a stern man and not always easy to approach, but he did at least speak to me on occasions about how well I was doing at increasing my sales budget and to keep up the good work. Something my direct sales manager rarely did.

When I saw the general manager and we discussed my wage issue, he called my manager into the meeting and told him to increase my wage and to also improve the relationship he had with me. After further discussion I was given a wage increase, but only marginally, and it was still not as much as the new person who was to be employed with the company. I didn't pursue it any further as I knew it would only make the relationship between my manager and I worse and, frankly, I wanted to keep my job. So, I let it go and accepted the fact I was on a lower wage than all the other men in the department.

After that I just kept my head down and my bum up working hard. I had built great relationships with my customer base. They all knew I was good at my job and that I would ensure their needs were met and all their orders were on time. I gave my manager no reason to question how or what I was doing when it came to my job.

There was one time I was called into his office, and he closed the door behind me. I remember thinking, *What the hell is going on here?* He started talking about my 'relationship' with one of the other men in the sales department. Garry (not his real name) and I got along well, but there were two other men in the department I also got along well with, mainly because they were younger than most of the others in the department (I was the youngest). Most were over forty-five years of age and at least six were in their fifties. I was twenty-seven when I got the job in the sales area, so I naturally gravitated to the younger men as we had more in common.

I have fond memories of the many laugh-out-loud moments with these two other men in the sales department and we were seen as a bit of a trio. When we were all in the office together, we would stand up and look over our partitions and nod to each other, indicating that it was smoko time. The laughs we had while outside having a smoke would often make others wonder what we were talking about. They both knew I wasn't easily offended and loved a good dirty joke; something that is frowned upon in a work environment today. I get that you have to be careful about what you say now and that it is difficult path to navigate when it comes to saying something considered 'inappropriate' I do think some banter is fine but you absolutely have to be careful of who you do this with.

Garry and I used to go and have lunch together at the local café down the road from the office (just like many other staff members). We didn't really do it that often as we were both out on the road seeing clients most of the time. Garry was a single man, whereas the other two men I hung out with were both married.

The reason I was called into the manager's office was because everyone was talking about my relationship with Garry. My manager asked me if anything was going on between us as he'd heard 'stories' about us. The first thing that came out of my mouth was, 'I am bloody married.' Not that being married stops some people from having office affairs, but I was shocked at his remarks. Naturally, I asked him what had been said and why people thought we were having an affair. Well, it was because we had lunch together. I mean really! We went out and lunched together at the local café where other workers also went so that constituted us having an affair.

I told the manager that nothing was going on, of course, but he replied that I had to be careful being seen together as the talk about me could impact my career. For God's sake! I was the only saleswoman in a department full of men, but I couldn't have lunch with any of them because I'd be talked about. When I did catch up with Garry for lunch after that it would be somewhere away from the office where nobody could see us. Garry was also spoken to about the rumours and obviously denied we were having an affair. Frankly, it was nobody's business, but when it comes to office gossip it is something you can't stop. Someone always likes to make up a good story.

I continued doing the job I was paid to do, and then after five years of being a sales executive I fell pregnant. I didn't inform the company until I was about three months pregnant, but one of the other salespeople I got along with made a comment one day that I wasn't going out for a ciggy and therefore I was probably pregnant. Little did he know, I was.

I had made the decision to try to get pregnant when I hit thirty. After about six months of trying and nothing happening, I thought my body was taking its time to get the contraceptive pill out of my system as I had been on it for twelve years. We both decided to have some tests, and I found out that I had endometriosis, a condition where the lining of the uterus (endometrium) grows outside of the uterus. It can lead to infertility in as many as 30 to 50 percent of those affected.

I had noticed that my periods were getting heavier, and I also had some cramping, but I just put it down to getting a bit older and thought nothing of it. Subsequently, I had to have a laparoscopy to remove the endometriosis cells from the lining of my uterus. I was relatively lucky as my endometriosis wasn't severe.

About four months after the procedure, I fell pregnant, and we were both overjoyed. We kept it a secret for three months and waited until after our second ultrasound to announce it, as I'd seen couples having to deal with telling everyone they'd had a miscarriage if it was announced too early. We just wanted to play it safe.

Our parents were thrilled for us and had wondered when we were going to have a child as we'd been married for almost ten years. Having a child was something I wanted, but I wasn't in a hurry.

After the ultrasound, and when I knew that everything was going well, I told my manager. He seemed happy for me and naturally asked what I was going to do when I had the baby. I informed him that I wanted to return to my position after having some time off to have the baby. Within a few months my maternity-leave replacement was hired, and I had to train him (yes, they employed another man). I was told that on my return to work, he would be placed into another area of Amcor.

In the two months before I was due to go on maternity leave, I was getting bigger and more tired. Spending so much time training someone was draining as well as having to keep up with my work. I was exhausted. I wanted to make sure he knew all my clients as it was important to me that they were looked after. One day I was going to return, and I didn't want to come back and clean up his mess.

About a month before I was due to leave, I could see that the new guy was struggling with learning everything. There was also the problem that the customer service person who looked after my clients was difficult to deal with. This person hated the job and it showed. As I had worked in the customer service section before I got promoted, I knew the job well. Most of the time I'd been doing her job as getting her to do anything was almost impossible. The customer service manager was well aware that she wasn't doing her job but every time she was spoken to about her performance, she broke down and cried.

The sales manager was about forty and couldn't handle having a 'mature woman' cry while being told that she wasn't doing her job. I lost count of how many times she was pulled into the office because customers were complaining about her. It was rather pathetic that they didn't just put her into another job that didn't deal directly with clients as she just couldn't handle the position. It was a demanding job and you had to keep on top of things, otherwise clients would lose their shit if their packaging wasn't received on time.

My replacement could see he was going to have problems dealing with his internal contact in customer service, and he actually complained to our sales manager about her as he could see firsthand she wasn't doing her job. Once again, she was pulled into the manager's office, cried, and it all went away. I know it would be difficult dealing with someone crying while you're telling them they aren't doing their job well, but the fact is that this is just what managers have to do from time to time. Not everyone is good at their job and that is a fact.

In my last two weeks a lot of my clients wanted to take me out for lunch. I was looking forward to being a bit spoiled by my clients and handing over most of my work to the new guy and starting to slow down, as I was really getting big. Just as I thought everything was in place, my replacement told me he'd been offered another job and that he wasn't going to stay. He was sorry that I'd spent so much time training him, but he just couldn't deal with the fact he was going to get little support internally, so he resigned.

I was devastated.

For the very first time, I cried in front of my manager. I had worked so hard to get everything in order and it all went up in smoke. He was also really disappointed because that meant trying to fill my position ASAP, which was not going to be easy. It was also a concern for my clients as they thought they would be left hanging without someone looking after them.

A couple of days later I had an appointment with my gynaecologist, and as much as everything was going great with the baby, he could see I was stressed. I told him about what had happened at work, so he gave me a doctor's certificate to state I was unfit to continue working. He advised that I should leave work as soon as possible. I was reluctant to do this but by then I only had two more weeks at work and only six weeks before the baby was due. I had done little when it came to preparing for the birth of my child, so I took his advice.

I contacted my clients and told them I was going on maternity leave two weeks earlier than expected. They were all great and knew that the whole situation with my replacement leaving was stressful. They all wished me well but were also disappointed I couldn't do lunch and have a proper goodbye with them. I had dealt with some of these clients for over five years, some of them for almost seven years as I had also dealt with them when I was in customer service.

Then I had to tell my boss.

He was not a happy camper.

He told me that I had to continue to do my job for the next two weeks as normal. When I gave him the doctor's certificate, he was stunned. I told him that I would be at home, and I had no problem being contacted if any information was required about my clients. In reality, I was leaving it way to close to the birth of my child to stay in the job. This sudden exit could have happened at any stage during my pregnancy if I'd had complications and, frankly, I had probably stayed longer than I should have. Blind Freddy could see I was huge.

A few days later, a woman from the customer service division was given the position of looking after my clients until my return. I had worked with her before and she was good at her job, so I was relieved she'd been picked. Shame that the company hadn't done this in the first place as it would have been a much easier handover to her than training a new person. In the following weeks I had her come to my place and go through various orders. I helped her a lot with information on my clients. It was great that she was so enthusiastic as it made me feel a lot happier that my clients were being looked after.

The secretary in the sales division organised a send-off at the office where I was given a voucher to purchase something for the baby. The inaugural coffee and cakes were organised, and I finally got to say goodbye to staff members. I felt weird leaving so quickly, but I had heaps to do at home getting the baby's room ready. For the next few weeks, that is what I did. My sister took me out shopping and I purchased a heap of things I needed. She had three children, so she knew what I required; she was a wonderful help.

The baby room was ready, and I felt that everything was organised. Now all I had to do was wait for the baby to be born.

Chapter 7

Maternity leave

On 6th January 1996, my husband's family had organised an 80th birthday surprise party for my father-in-law. It was held at my sister-in-law's house and a marquee was set up and lots of food was prepared. My husband obviously helped out a lot with the setup and leading up to the Saturday night he was running around like a madman trying to get it organised. The party went off without a hitch, and I remember walking around that night handing out food.

The following morning while lying in bed I felt a few little niggles in the stomach region but said nothing, and we both got up to have breakfast early as my husband needed to pull down the marquee at his sister's house and return it. We were having our breakfast and I had a bigger niggle and thought to myself that this baby could be on its way.

My husband got up from the table and said, 'Well, I'd better get moving and return the marquee.'

I said, 'I don't know if you should.'

'Why?'

'I think the baby might be coming.'

Stunned silence.

He said, 'Are you sure?'

'I've had a couple of niggles so I think you might need to hang around.'

'I have to get this bloody marquee back!'

I was thinking, *Fuck the marquee*. But I said, 'Well, I think you're going to have to get someone else to do that.'

He phoned his sister and told her what was happening, and she was excited that the baby was on its way.

Standing up and walking around the previous night had obviously brought things on. I wasn't concerned at all as I was fairly big and, being the middle of summer, I was pretty keen to get this baby out. It was only two weeks early, so it wasn't really a big deal. For the next six hours my contractions became closer and closer, and we finally made the call to the hospital to say we were coming in.

When we got to the hospital, everything was going along well. My husband was a bit stressed as he had been busy all week setting up for his father's birthday party and, subsequently, he was suffering with gout in his big toe. He was limping around and doing a bit of complaining, which was probably not really appropriate considering I was about to give birth, and I had to remind him of that a few times.

My contractions started to stall, and the nurse could see that my husband was struggling to deal with the pain from the gout, so she gave him some painkillers and told him to have a rest in another room. Probably a good thing as he needed to get some rest before the real action started.

After about twelve hours, everything really slowed down and my contractions didn't progress. Once it got to sixteen hours I was asked if I wanted an epidural as I was exhausted. I reluctantly decided to have one. It is a scary thing having a needle injected into your back while trying not to move, so it was timed for when I wasn't having a contraction. I had heard horror stories about epidurals going wrong, so I was relieved when it was done without a hitch.

While lying on the bed, I watched the machine that was monitoring my contractions. I saw it spike upwards yet felt nothing. I thought that I should have done this hours ago as I felt no pain at all; it was bloody terrific. When my contractions were getting closer and I was fully dilated, I was told to start pushing; a hard thing to do when you can't feel a bloody thing below your waist.

My gynaecologist arrived and he was ready to get into action for the delivery. I was told to push and do an action like you're trying to have a massive shit. I thought that was hilarious but did as they said. My gynaecologist told me that if I didn't push harder, I would have to go to the operating theatre and have a caesarean, so I pushed as hard as I could, which is so difficult when you can't feel your actions.

Finally, after twenty-one hours, our beautiful son was born. Yes, a long, difficult labour and close to being a caesarean delivery, but I finally had him naturally, with the help of an epidural.

When our son came into the world, he screamed for about an hour, which was a massive distraction considering I was being sewn up. Luckily, the epidural meant I couldn't feel anything, but then when it wore off it was a different story. A lot of sewing up was required and I was in agony; the pain was unbearable, so I was given strong painkillers. This was a good thing at first but, unfortunately, they made me very constipated.

My sister told me to ask the nurses for a frozen condom, which is a condom full of frozen water. You put them on your vagina (not into it) to cool it down and stop the burning. I thought it was a bit silly until I used one; what a bloody relief, but they melted so quickly, obviously due to the extreme heat.

I was in a room with another woman on the first night, and she'd just had her first baby as well. I told her about the frozen condoms, and I could hear her sigh with relief when she placed it onto her vagina. While dealing with a burning vagina you also have to attend to a period from hell. Maternity pads feel like you're wearing a nappy; they are horrible but unfortunately necessary. I thought I was going to bleed to death at one stage but after about six days it tapered off, though didn't completely stop for ten days. Yes, the period from hell.

After the first night, I was moved to a private room. It was lovely to have my own room and because we had private health cover I was staying in a nice, private hospital. The ward was newly built, and it felt like a hotel room. The food was nice as well and my husband stayed a couple of times and had dinner with me. He was still working at the time and had organised time off when the baby came home. Back in 1996 he had to take time off his holiday leave as paternity leave wasn't available.

While in the hospital, I had many nurses attend to me. Some were lovely and attentive, but I also had one nurse (we'll call her Nurse R) who clearly shouldn't have been in a maternity ward.

I was having a lot of difficulty breastfeeding. I had lots of milk and my boobs were so big I thought they were going to explode. At first it was thought that I might have mastitis, which is a painful condition where your milk ducts get blocked, causing infection. I was put on a breast pump and slowly, slowly, my milk started to come through. My breasts were so sore that I put refrigerated cabbage leaves on them to ease the pain.

So, I had frozen condoms on my vagina and cold cabbage leaves on my breasts. Oh, the joys of having a baby!

One night I had Nurse R attend to me while I was trying to breastfeed. She was pushing my son onto my breast, and he was getting stressed out and so was I. I was getting so pissed off that I almost punched her lights out. I finally told her to leave and not come back. I had another nurse come and see me and by this stage I was in tears. She took my son to the nursery and told me to try to get some sleep. They had some of my breastmilk stored away in the nursery, so they took over and fed my son. The next morning, I went to the nursery and got my son, took him back to the room and tried to breastfeed but it was a slow process, and it was not a 'natural' thing for me.

A massive machine (not just a small hand pump) was brought into my room to try to pump the milk, and that is when I felt like a cow. Finally, my milk started to come through and I could feed my son normally, but I needed industrial-strength machinery to get it happening. I remember when my husband came into the room and saw me; the look on his face said it all. It was obviously confronting for him to see his wife on a massive milk pump, and I can assure you I wasn't a happy camper.

Due to the painkillers, I hadn't had a bowel movement for about a week, and I felt like I was going to have another baby. The thought of having a massive poo was daunting considering I'd been sewn up. I thought the stitches might tear apart, and I would never get out of this hospital. I was finally given a suppository and the next day, to my great relief, I had the biggest poo. I can't begin to tell you how good I felt and that everything stayed intact.

Due to the number of stitches I'd received (I never asked how many but I know it was a lot), I had the nurses constantly checking me to ensure I wasn't getting an infection. I recall one nurse coming into my room to check the equipment downstairs and she looked like a rabbit staring into headlights; the look on her face said it all. She said, 'Now that's what I call a bruise.' She stopped herself from saying more but it was obvious that it was pretty messy. Wishing she had kept her thoughts to herself, I then began to wonder just how bad my vagina looked and if I was ever going to have sex again. At this stage I was too scared to take a look; I was dealing with enough at the time.

A lot of women say that when you give birth, once you're given that beautiful bundle of joy you forget about how painful the delivery was. That may be true for some women who breeze through childbirth, but I think for the large majority you don't forget. I didn't have the pain of a delivery because of the epidural but I most certainly remember what I had to deal with after giving birth and how much pain I was in due to tearing. The fact that twenty-five years on I can still remember my time in hospital tells you that I haven't forgotten, and I don't believe for one second I am alone.

After nine days, I finally left the hospital and we brought our beautiful boy home. This was wonderful as we could both finally spend time looking after him. It was a special but challenging time adjusting to life with a newborn, and when it is your first child the adjustments are massive.

Coming home from hospital seemed strange as we had a little bundle of joy with us. Thank God I hadn't gone full term with my pregnancy as my boy was delivered at 8.1 pounds (3.6 kg), so he was more than big enough. I was also still sore in the downstairs department and still unable to sit properly. I used to lean on one of my bum cheeks for weeks after I gave birth. It took me two months before I had enough courage to get a mirror to have a look, and I was relieved to find everything looked fine!

The first six weeks were hard, even though my boy was pretty good in the whole scheme of things. I breastfed for about three months and slowly converted him to formula as my boobs were still so sore. When feeding, he was like a vacuum cleaner on my nipples, and they just couldn't take it anymore. I felt bad about putting him on formula as you're told that you should breastfeed for as long as possible. He was nice and chubby plus content with life, sleeping well, so all was good in the world.

At the age of thirty-two I was glad that I'd finally had a child as leaving it any longer could have made getting pregnant more difficult.

As we knew I'd be taking time off to look after the baby, we'd started saving so that we had extra money in the bank while I wasn't earning an income. We didn't want to be skimping and worrying about being able to pay the mortgage and the bills with only one wage. The thought of getting paid while on maternity leave never entered my mind as I wasn't going to be working and that was that.

When it comes to paid maternity leave, it wasn't available to me, or my mother or any other woman in my family for that fact. It was just a given that when a woman fell pregnant, she would leave work. That is just the way it was back then before the *Maternity Leave Act* came into effect.

*The Maternity Leave Act came into effect in 1973 and provided 12 weeks of paid leave to female Commonwealth employees **only** (0.4% of the total female workforce).*

Back in 1973, few women were eligible for paid maternity leave as many weren't working at all. During the 1960s, women working in the public service and in many private companies were forced to resign from their jobs when they got married. Working while pregnant would not have been thought of at all.

Finally, in 1979, all female employees working on a long-term basis (twelve months or more) were entitled to 52 weeks' unpaid maternity leave. Almost twenty years later, in 1990, the Industrial Relations Commission ruled that 51 weeks of unpaid parental leave after the birth of a child could be taken by either parent. Why it was changed from 52 to 51 is anyone's guess.

It was another twenty-two years later that paid maternity leave was introduced.[13]

The Paid Parental Leave scheme is based on recommendations made in the 2009 Productivity Commission Inquiry Report into Paid Parental Leave (Productivity Commission, 2009), and was

---

[13] https://www.fairwork.gov.au/leave/maternity-and-parental-leave

introduced on 1 January 2011. It provides 18 weeks of Parental Leave Pay at the rate of the national minimum wage (currently $606.50 per week before tax) for the primary carer, usually the birth mother. The primary carer may transfer some or all of their unused Parental Leave Pay to an eligible partner.

To be eligible for maternity leave, you must have worked for the company for twelve months or more. A position in the company must also be available to you on your return to work after a maximum of twelve months of being on maternity leave.

Lots of things have changed when it comes to women in the workforce today: women comprise roughly 47 percent of all employees in Australia, and due to the high cost of living in Australia it is almost impossible for many people to pay a home mortgage off unless both partners are working.

Maternity leave is a time for parents to bond with their baby, but the reality is that the mother is always going to take time off to have a baby because she is the one actually giving birth. She needs time for her body to heal and her hormones to settle. If she chooses to breastfeed this is also a challenge for some women as it doesn't always come naturally, as I found out. Breastfeeding can become stressful as some women are judged poorly when they don't breastfeed, and they are sometimes seen as not doing the right thing by the child.

Women can be so hard on each other when it comes to child rearing.

Because men earn more money than women it makes sense for the woman to use all the maternity leave, and it is uncommon for men to take paternity leave. It does happen but only one in twenty men take paternity leave.

I can look back now and see that with all the difficulties I went through giving birth and the complications I had, I was starting to fall into a dark hole of depression. I didn't get any psychological help as I didn't see back then that I needed it. Even though we knew about postnatal depression, it was rarely spoken about, and my guess would be that it wasn't spoken about because you would be seen as failing as a mother.

The cause of postnatal depression is not fully understood even today. It can be attributed to a combination of environmental, emotional, hormonal and genetic factors. Sleep deprivation may worsen symptoms or increase the likelihood of the condition. Let's face it, sleep deprivation is a given when you have a baby.

Below is a list of factors that contribute to postnatal depression:

- Drop in hormone levels after the delivery
- Family history of depression
- Emotional issues such as stress between partners or family
- Stressful events during pregnancy
- Complications during childbirth
- Lack of help/support

When I look at this list, I had all of these things, but most women say that it's just what you have to deal with when having a child and you just have to suck it up.

When you have your baby, it's arranged for you to attend child health centres where you meet other mothers and have discussions with qualified health professionals. These discussions were mainly around feeding and sleeping routines and also looking for signs of anything that may be wrong with your child and picking up on illnesses. I recall some mothers having problems with babies crying all night and they clearly had sleep deprivation, but postnatal depression was never really spoken about much; it was more about the baby, not the mother. Some mothers seemed to be coping well and, frankly, they made you feel inadequate, but my guess is that most of them put up a good front.

All of these changes in your life when you have a baby are massive. Not only does the body have to mend, but so does the mind. Having a child changes your life so much and you have to make a lot of adjustments, which can be difficult. You have to also deal with the financial challenges, which can cause extra stress. Most people plan to have a family, as we did, and knowing you can return to your job is something that you should be able to rely on. In my case, I had worked for the company for almost seven years by this point.

As much as I had my difficulties when my son was a baby, I also had a lot of joy. I won't deny that I missed my job and the interaction with clients and work colleagues, but I loved my son to bits. They grow so quickly and before you know it they're walking and talking and their personality is showing through.

When I fell pregnant, I booked a place in a local childcare centre just around the corner from home. It was a new centre and the woman who ran it was lovely. You needed to book early (more than a year in advance in most cases) when it came to childcare otherwise you wouldn't get into one when trying to return to work. Well, you could, but some of the childcare facilities I saw you wouldn't put your dog in.

So, we were all set, my husband and I had saved money to prepare for the loss in wages while I was off work, and I also had my son booked into a childcare centre so I could return to work. I had done everything possible to make my life less stressful when having a baby so that I could return to work and continue my career.

You can have the best laid plans, but something often comes along and pulls the rug from under you.

Chapter 8

Back to work

On Friday, 14th June 1996, I phoned my manager to make an appointment to see him regarding my return to work. In this conversation he said he was going to call me to attend an announcement at the Box Hill office at 11am on Monday the 17th. I did think it was rather strange that after being on maternity leave for six months, the day I called him to discuss my return to work he said he was thinking of calling me. I knew something was going on, but I also thought that maybe the company was keen to get me back on board.

When I arrived at the office on Monday 17th June, most of the sales team had left the building as the announcement had been made earlier. What time that was, I actually didn't find out. I was told by other staff members that the Brooklyn and Box Hill branches were going to be amalgamated and that four people had already been made redundant. Even at this stage I honestly believed my job was safe as when I left to go on maternity leave, I was told that I could return to my position. The fact that it was actually the law to do this didn't enter my mind. I knew I was good at my job and the company really had no valid reason to fire me or make me redundant. My skills in sales were of a high standard and that is why my sales had tripled in the time I had worked for the company.

I got along well with the HR manager at the Box Hill branch, so I went to see her about what was going on, and she looked rattled. We had a discussion about some of the people that were dismissed and wondered why some others had not been let go as it was well known they were not good at their jobs. But it came down to money. Staff who'd worked with the company for anything from ten to twenty-five years would have had huge redundancy payouts. In fact, none of the people who had worked there for more than ten years were made redundant. She didn't let on at all about what was going to happen to me, but she must have known as she was the HR manager for the branch, after all.

She kept silent.

Just after 11am, the general manager's secretary asked me to go upstairs into the main office. I hadn't met the new general manager, and I assumed he wanted to meet me. She led me into an office where my direct sales manager and another man from the HR division at head office in Camberwell (who I had never met before) were sitting. They both stood up, shook my hand and we all sat down. That is when my heart started to beat a little faster.

My manager read straight from notes on the desk, like a speech, but in a cold, monotone voice. He stated that due to the amalgamation of the two branches, my position had been made redundant. He continued to say more but the words were not sinking in as my head was spinning at the word 'redundant'. I sat in stunned silence without any words coming out of my mouth. I must have looked like a rabbit staring into headlights on the side of the road. I then stood up and said, 'Thank you very much, gentlemen,' and proceeded to walk out of the office. The other man in the office stood up from his chair and let me pass. Neither of them said anything, they just let me walk out even though they could clearly see I was starting to cry.

I walked along the hallway and down the stairs to the sales office. I was in complete shock. As the sales office had been deserted due to the announcement, I went and spoke to the secretary in the sales area and told her what had happened. I was distraught by this stage. She comforted me and asked if I was okay to drive home, and I said I would be fine, but I was far from it. I really don't know how I managed to drive home at all as my head was spinning.

I called my husband about what had happened; he was shocked as well. As our son was being minded by my in-laws, he arranged to pick him up after work so that I had some time to get myself together before my son came home. After I'd calmed down, and the reality of what had occurred had sunk in, I decided to call my manager to find out more about why I had been chosen for redundancy.

When I left the company to go on maternity leave, a woman from the customer service division was placed into my position. The only thing I wanted to know was, did my replacement keep her job? When I asked him this question he said, 'Yes.' I then went on to say, 'How can my replacement keep her job when in fact it was my job she had been given while I was on maternity leave?' He said that the area I was looking after had been changed around and my replacement had taken over one of the other areas. So, even though all the territories in the Melbourne area had been amalgamated, my area no longer existed! Of course, it bloody well did. It wasn't like the suburbs I looked after had disappeared into space; it had just been made into a bigger sales territory, and guess who was looking after it – my replacement. He then said that he didn't get the chance to give me my paycheque and that he would arrange for it to be delivered to my house. I didn't continue the conversation as I might have said something I would later regret.

Frankly, he'd had more than enough time to give me my cheque and discuss my redundancy in the office. It wasn't like I had run out of there, bolted down the hall and left the building straight away. He could have stopped me from leaving the meeting and explained, in a humane manner, why I was chosen, or get someone to check on me before I left the building as I was clearly upset. I was in the sales office for about twenty minutes before I left the building. Instead, he did nothing. I had worked with this man for almost seven years, and he showed absolutely no empathy to me at all. It was a bonus to him that I left the office as he avoided being asked questions face to face.

The HR person that was in the office was clearly there as a witness to the proceedings. He said nothing as he moved his chair to allow me to pass. Here is a person supposedly qualified in human resources and to deal with 'human' issues, but he didn't care about my welfare either.

The next day my paycheque arrived. I had to sign for it to prove I had received it.

On 24th June 1996, I made the decision to contact the executive director of operations, who was high up on the ladder when it came to making the decisions on operational matters. He listened to what I had to say and advised me to write a letter to the general manager of HR and also the general manager of Victoria, who'd been appointed to this position while I was on maternity leave. At the end of this conversation, he said, 'Don't spend too much money on legal costs.' It was only then that I realised I should look into possibly making a claim for unfair dismissal.

I sent a letter to both of the men he referred to and asked for more clarification regarding my position, and how I could be made redundant while on maternity leave when my replacement kept her job. I would like to point out at this stage that my replacement was a much older woman who was at an age where she would not be having any more children.

I received a letter from the general manager of HR stating:

Dear Linda,

The purpose of this letter is to acknowledge receipt of your correspondence dated the 1st July 1996 and to clarify a misunderstanding you appear to have regarding your redundancy.

We understand that you feel very disappointed about your position being made redundant at Amcor Fibre Packaging and wish to advise that the reorganisation of our sales and administration in Victoria has resulted in many employees losing their employment, including people like yourself who were previously in sales.

You made mention in your covering letter that you were unclear why your position had been made redundant because the person who replaced you was still working in your position. It may help to lessen your concerns to learn that the position you previously held no longer exists, as a result of the reorganisation of our sales and administration functions of Victoria.

Again, we deeply regret your concerns and assure you all the appropriate steps have been taken to ensure that your redundancy was justified and conducted in a fair and even-handed manner.

Yours sincerely,

Well, that didn't really explain why I was chosen, and as for being fair and even handed? I don't think so.

That is when I called Slater and Gordon Lawyers to make an appointment to see them. As the first appointment is free, I saw no reason not to go down this path. I had to go into Melbourne to meet with them. After going through everything and what had happened to me, I knew I had strong grounds to take this matter further.

Chapter 9

Going to court

On 2nd August 1996, I received a letter from Slater and Gordon confirming they would represent me for my unfair dismissal claim. Not really understanding the complexity of the filing for unfair dismissal, I just accepted what they were doing and went along with their instructions.

A conciliation conference was listed at the Australian Industrial Relations Commission on Thursday 15th August 1996 at 3.30pm. This meeting was so that both parties could discuss my claim and possibly come up with some type of agreement. I had my solicitor with me, and Amcor had a person from their HR department (whom I had never met before) and a legal representative. The first thing Amcor brought up was that this claim was made outside the fourteen days to make an unfair dismissal claim, and therefore I didn't really have a leg to stand on. Further discussion took place on what led to my dismissal, and then the conciliator took both parties into separate rooms to try to get more information.

It was stressful sitting opposite these men as it was intimidating and their demeanour felt aggressive. The conciliator went from office to office and this went on for about an hour before, finally, the conciliator came back to my solicitor and informed us that we had a strong case. Amcor were informed of this, but they were sticking to the fact my claim had been made outside the fourteen days that was required by the Industrial Relations Commission to make a claim for unfair dismissal.

The reason I had taken more than fourteen days was because of the letters I had written to the company and I had waited on their replies. It was only after I had received the letter from Amcor, which told me nothing about the process of how I had been picked, that I made my claim for unfair dismissal.

When the meeting was over, I walked into the hallway and started to cry. I had held that in for so long, and the intimidation of the whole situation had finally got to me. I went to the toilet and regained my composure and then quickly spoke to my solicitor. She informed me that they had to lodge a claim for an extension of time with the Commission. I thought then that it was all over, but to my surprise, on 28th August 1996, the extension was granted and my claim for unfair dismissal could go ahead.

I tried to envision what was going on behind closed doors at Amcor and how they might all be shitting themselves that the extension had been granted when they all thought it was a done deal that I had no claim. Now, they were going to have to get their act together and defend themselves against a woman!

Various letters went back and forth between solicitors on both sides and, of course, they kept to the line that the reason for my dismissal was due to a restructure of the company because of 'operational requirements'.

On 1st October 1996, I was advised that a hearing at the Industrial Relations Court had been set down for the 19th and 20th February 1997. There was no further discussion regarding my hearing until a couple of days prior to 19th February.

17th February 1997 was a crazy day with phone calls from my solicitor to Amcor's solicitors before, finally, I was offered some 'shut-up' money. It was $10,000. I told my solicitor to tell them, 'They can take their $10,000 and stick it where the sun doesn't shine.' I am sure she didn't actually say this to them, but it meant we were off to court and a barrister would be brought in to defend me with the proceedings.

Later that day I had a call from a person at Amcor's Box Hill office. They knew something was going down and it was to do with me. Apparently, the boardroom was full of management and solicitors discussing their next move, which was obviously facing me in a courtroom and facing a judge, plus being questioned about how they came to pick me for redundancy. This person wished me good luck but also indicated that Amcor was very concerned about this going to court and the fact I had rejected their 'shut-up' offer.

Shut-up money is just that. Money offered to you and then you sign a document that says you cannot discuss what occurred regarding your dismissal, *ever*. Having an extra $10,000 would have come in handy, but I wanted the truth to come out; it was never about the money.

On the morning of 19th February, while sitting with my solicitor just before going into court, the sick feeling inside me just kept rising, and I was thinking, *What the hell have I done? Is this really worth it?* I saw the legal team representing Amcor pile into the courtroom and my stomach tightened up to a point where I felt like I was going to throw up. They had a legal team of four, and I had one solicitor and one barrister. I knew then that this was going to be a very long day.

Just before entering the courtroom, my barrister, whom I had only spoken to for the first time the day before going to court, asked me to sign a form stating I was aware that my case had no precedent. Essentially, they could not refer to any previous cases like mine that had been through the court system regarding being made redundant while on maternity leave because they didn't exist. I vaguely remember just signing the document and just wanting to get it all over and done with. I really didn't know at the time what it meant that there was no precedent and how that would affect my case.

Slater and Gordon's catch-cry was 'No win, no pay', but I don't think they thought it would go to court either. The reason I had only spoken to my barrister the day before court was because one had not been allocated. Slater and Gordon obviously thought I would just take the shut-up money too.

Two days were allocated to my case, but I was told it was unlikely that it would go for that long. As Amcor was the respondent, they went first with defending themselves in court, so I had to sit back and hear their version of events and the reason for my dismissal. Various managers were brought in to testify and, notably, the general manager, whom I had never met as he joined the company when I was on maternity leave, had to justify why I was made redundant. He wasn't happy about being brought into this courtroom. As the final decision was his regarding who was let go, it was not a good look that he had never met me before. How could someone make the final decision about me being made redundant when they didn't even know who I was let alone whether I was any good at my job or not? He did finally admit that he had relied on his management team's advice when making the final decision.

My direct manager was brought in, and he got a bit of a grilling. I recall he made the comment that he got along well with me and considered us to have a good working relationship. I will admit that we were never really at loggerheads; we did have our different views on certain things, but I think that is only natural. The only time I remember it getting heated between us was when I was about to go on maternity leave and my replacement had resigned. Although I decided to take my doctor's advice and leave earlier than expected, I had put everything in place to ensure my customers were being looked after.

Now was the time for Amcor management to explain their actions, and that was why I was in the courtroom. I wanted to hear what they had to say; I wanted to know how they came to this decision even though there were laws in place to protect me, which they had obviously ignored.

The proceedings went on until lunchtime, and then it was my turn to take the stand.

When you get onto the stand you have to swear on a bible or do an affirmation. An affirmation is when you don't have a religious background and you don't want to swear on a bible. I chose to do an affirmation and swear that I was telling the truth. As I'm not a religious person, I didn't see the sense in swearing on a bible I didn't believe in.

I got an absolute grilling from Amcor's legal team. The four of them all took turns to try to rattle me; it was truly horrible. I did start to cry at one stage as it just became overwhelming, and we took a short break before coming back to the courtroom. I am sure at this stage Amcor's legal team must have thought they'd cracked me, but I came back to the stand having regained my composure and was ready for the next onslaught. This continued for a couple of hours. They did their best to discredit me, but I answered everything to the best of my knowledge and tried hard not to lose my shit again.

At around 4pm the judge called an end to the proceedings for the day, but we hadn't finished, so therefore we were going to continue into the second day. I remember thinking in the morning that this would be over at the end of the day, and I could go home and have a stiff drink and just wait for the judge to make her decision. My legal team was thrilled we got this judge as she had a good reputation for being thorough. I have no doubt that Amcor's legal team was not happy we had a female judge.

The second day was just as awful. The drive into Melbourne felt like déjà vu as I hadn't thought I would be heading back to the courtroom to be grilled again.

The proceedings went for another couple of hours and some of the questions seemed completely irrelevant, like when they asked me why I'd sworn on a bible when I signed paperwork at my solicitor's office, yet I didn't swear on the bible in the courtroom. They obviously had this paperwork for the case and tried to make out I was lying because I didn't swear on a bible. I didn't get to answer this question as the judge interjected and said, 'This case is not about the applicant's religious beliefs,' and dismissed the questioning. I did recall swearing on a bible at my solicitor's office, and when I did that, I actually said to my solicitor, 'Seems strange to swear on the bible when I'm not a religious person.' I hadn't known you could just do an affirmation, and if I had known, that is what I would have done.

They also wanted to push the issue that I'd refused to work until the end of my original finish date before going on maternity leave. When my barrister submitted the doctor's certificate to the judge, the questions on the lines that I didn't want to work were also dismissed.

Just before lunch, the questioning finally ended and the judge wrapped everything up. It was finally over. After another three hours of questioning, I could finally breathe.

I will admit that my full recollection now of those two days in court is largely a bit of a blur. It was twenty-five years ago now, but the one thing I do remember is feeling like I was the one who had done the wrong thing by Amcor, and that I wasn't good at my job. I was made to feel like I was at fault, that I was the horrible person who was just being a troublemaker for lodging an unfair dismissal claim.

I'd started seeing a psychologist after I was dismissed from Amcor as I was unable to comprehend what had happened to me, and I also think I was dealing with postnatal depression. Like most first-time mothers, having a baby can be overwhelming. On top of that, losing a job that I loved just added to my depression. I had all the signs of postnatal depression but couldn't see it as I was consumed by my dismissal.

I was never really treated for postnatal depression as most of my sadness seemed to be from losing my job and going through a court process. I was probably mad to go through something like that when I'd just had a baby, but my mind was set on proving I was discriminated against just for having a baby. I totally get why women take the 'shut-up money' and focus on their child and, unfortunately, that is what most companies know a mother will probably do and therefore bury the issue of discrimination. Clearly, I was not one of those mothers, but I also respect their decision to do so.

I had to wait two months for the judge to make her decision. Every week felt like a month, and I thought I would never get any answers. I was depressed, and I felt a lack of support from family and friends who thought I was mad to take Amcor on. It was all clearly taking a toll on me and waiting for the decision only made it worse. I thought, *When this is all over, I will be fine*. But this was only the start of my journey into depression and anxiety. Little did I know how much my life would change and the path I was now on.

Chapter 10

The decision

I never went into the court case for the sake of money. It was all about standing up for the truth. I wanted Amcor to be held accountable for their decision to make me redundant, and for not taking into account the laws that existed to protect women when they've had a baby and want to return to their jobs.

On 2nd May 1997, almost one year after I was made redundant, the judge finally made her decision. Amcor and I had to return to the courtroom to hear her decision being read out. While waiting for our turn to enter the courtroom, the HR manager that I'd first met at the conciliation meeting was also there. In the waiting area he came up to me and introduced himself. I was taken aback that he did this. I said to him, 'I'm surprised that anyone from Amcor would be here for this.' He said, 'Amcor is very interested in knowing about the decision.' Then we were called in.

My solicitor was with me and, as the judge read out the decision, she smiled at me when it was stated that Amcor was in contravention of s170DC, s170DE (1), S170DF (1) (f) and s170DF (1) (g) of the *Industrial Relations Act*:

170DC. An employer must not terminate an employee's employment for reasons related to the employee's conduct or performance unless:

(a) the employee has been given the opportunity to defend himself or herself against the allegations made; or

(b) the employer could not reasonably be expected to give the employee that opportunity.

170DE. (1) An employer must not terminate an employee's employment unless there is a valid reason, or valid reasons, connected with the employee's capacity or conduct or based on the operational requirements of the undertaking, establishment or service.

170DF. (1) An employer must not terminate an employee's employment for any one or more of the following reasons, or for reasons including any one or more of the following reasons:

(f) race, colour, sex, sexual preference, age, physical or mental disability, marital status, family responsibilities, pregnancy, religion, political opinion, national extraction or social origin;

(g) absence from work during maternity leave or other parental leave.

The judge didn't read out her whole decision, but we were given a typed copy of the reasons for her decision. It is a fifteen-page document that goes into great detail.

I felt like a stunned mullet all day, like it wasn't real. It was finally over, and I could move on. I really didn't know how to feel as, in the back of my mind, I thought I wouldn't win, and all of this was going to be a waste of time. Self-doubt had crept in.

Once I got home and had time to really read the decision and take it all in, I found it was a very damning decision towards Amcor and its processes regarding selection for redundancy.

Page 6 of the decision read:

... I do not accept that it was an operational requirement that the applicant's employment be terminated ...

... evidence was that the respondent selected the applicant for redundancy on the basis that she was alleged "not to be a team player" *and* "there had been some difficulties between her and the manager". *I do not accept that there is evidence in these proceedings to support the contention that the applicant was not a* "team player"*......the Applicant's supervisor and Sales Manager, was equivocal as to his evidence in relation to this aspect of the applicant's performance. ...*

... Her salary review appraisals confirm that in the most recent review she was assessed at a performance level well in excess of other employees who were retained.

Page 9 of the decision read:

It was the negative view of her capabilities, held by the sales manager, that was the reason why she was selected for redundancy.

I had taken on a large, male-dominated corporation and won. I was brave enough to stand up to them and not be intimidated (even though I was on many occasions) and bullied. I was offered money to go away and never talk about what happened. It was not easy by any stretch of the imagination, but I had done it, and I felt vindicated.

Everything Amcor had said about me were lies, and the truth had finally come out.

The following document is the full, unaltered case decision, sourced directly from
http://www.austlii.edu.au/au/cases/cth/IRCA/1997/153.html

(My surname at the time I lodged this claim was Jordan and due to court error my surname is typed Jordon throughout this document)

Jordan v Amcor Limited [1997] IRCA 153 (2 May 1997)

Last Updated: 18 August 2009

DECISION NO:153/97

CATCHWORDS

INDUSTRIAL LAW - complaint of UNLAWFUL TERMINATION -

whether VALID REASON - whether termination for OPERATIONAL REQUIREMENT - whether objective selection criteria for REDUNDANCY - whether termination for PROHIBITED REASON - whether applicant given OPPORTUNITY TO RESPOND - REMEDY - on-going losses -

Workplace Relations Act 1996 ss170DE(1), 170DC, 170DF(1)(f), 170DF(1)(g),

170EA, 170EE(3)

Workplace Relations Act 1996 Schedule 14

Bechara v Harrison Healey &Co <u>(1996) 65 IR 382</u>

Termination, Change & Redundancy Case [1984] AILR 256

JORDON -V- AMCOR LIMITED

VI 2256 of 1996

Before : PARKINSON JR

Place : MELBOURNE

Date : 2 MAY 1997

IN THE INDUSTRIAL RELATIONS COURT

OF AUSTRALIA

VICTORIA DISTRICT REGISTRY

VI 2256 of 1996

B E T W E E N:

Linda JORDON

Applicant

A N D

AMCOR LIMITED

Respondent

MINUTES OF ORDERS

2 MAY 1997 PARKINSON JR

THE COURT ORDERS THAT:

1. The respondent pay to the applicant compensation in the sum of $7174.40 pursuant to Section 170EE(3) of the <u>Workplace Relations Act, 1996</u>.

2. Such payment be made within 21 days of this Order.

IN THE INDUSTRIAL RELATIONS COURT

OF AUSTRALIA

VICTORIA DISTRICT REGISTRY

VI 2256 of 1996

B E T W E E N:

Linda JORDON

Applicant

A N D

AMCOR LIMITED

Respondent

REASONS FOR DECISION

2 MAY 1997 PARKINSON JR

This is a decision in an application made pursuant to Section 170EA of the <u>Workplace Relations Act 1996</u>. The applicant

commenced employment with the respondent on 28 March,
1989. She was initially employed as a Customer Services Clerk
with APM Containers Ltd Scoresby, however in February 1991
she was appointed to the position of Territory Sales
Representative with Amcor Fibre Packaging Division. She
remained in that position until the termination of her
employment effective 19 June, 1996. The termination of her
employment occurred during the course of her absence from the
workplace on maternity leave.

The respondent manufactures and sells corrugated packaging,
including boxes, partitions and displays to industrial users and
end users. Product is also sold for the purpose of conversion into
boxes and packaging. The respondent operates two relevant sites
in Victoria. One site is at Box Hill where the applicant was
located and the other site is at Brooklyn. Those sites operated as
separately managed and administered sites with both operating
separate sales teams and management structures, until mid 1996.
As I will discuss later in this judgment, various structural and
organisational changes were made to those operations by a
decision made in March 1996.

The applicant contends that the termination of her employment
was without valid reason and contravened s170DE(1),
s170DF(1)(f) and s170DF(1)(g) of the Act. She contends that
there was no operational requirement that she be made redundant
at the time the termination of her employment occurred and
further contends she was selected for redundancy for the reason
of, or partly for the reason of, her sex, and pregnancy and/or on
account of her absence from work on authorised maternity leave.

The respondent contends that the termination of the employment was for valid reason arising from the operational requirements of the business and that the termination was not for the reason and nor did it include the reason the applicant's sex, marital status or pregnancy. The respondent contends that objective selection criteria was used in the selection of the employees who were to be made redundant.

In 1995 the applicant advised the respondent of her pregnancy and her intention to take maternity leave. As a consequence of this advice the respondent advertised for and hired a short term replacement employee for the applicant's position. The applicant, in the period shortly before leaving on maternity leave, assisted the replacement employee in establishing himself in the area. The replacement employee advised he was resigning shortly before the applicant was due to commence her scheduled maternity leave. The applicant was anxious about this resignation and in particular concerned to ensure that her clients would be adequately serviced during her absence. An alternative replacement employee was obtained, that employee being promoted from her existing employment in the respondent. The respondent's evidence was that the appointment whilst initially designed to cover the applicant's territory during her absence, was always intended to result in a permanent appointment for that employee to a sales position, after the applicant had returned to her position.

The applicant commenced the leave, including some annual leave, in November, 1995 some 2 weeks earlier than originally planned owing to doctors advice. Her evidence was that she intended to return to her employment at the end of the period of maternity leave on 3 January, 1997. The applicant's child was born on 8 January, 1996.

During the applicant's absence on maternity leave a restructure
of the operations was announced. This restructure came about as
a result of a meeting of managers held on 15 and 16 March,
1996. Further meetings occurred in May and June 1996 wherein
the detail of the structures and staffing were considered. In the
course of the meetings there had been a decision taken to
amalgamate the structural and reporting responsibilities of the
Box Hill and Brooklyn facilities and consequently to reorganise
all of the sales areas. The Melbourne and Country regions had
been previously divided into 40 regions, with those regions being
allocated and serviced by Box Hill or Brooklyn. As a result of
the reorganisation, the regions were altered, some abolished and
some expanded to encompass existing regions. This process
resulted in there being 34 regions, six less than had previously
existed. The management team then allocated the regions
amongst the staff. Included in the staff numbers available for
allocation of areas, were all of the existing occupants of
permanent positions, including the applicant, the employee who
replaced the applicant during her maternity leave and another
employee who was transferred from the customer service area
into a sales consultant position effective 17 June, 1996. Evidence
was called as to the actual effect of these changes. As a
consequence of these changes a number of positions for sales
consultants were determined to be redundant. The selection
criteria for determining who was to be appointed was vague and
unclear as to detail or measurement. The evidence is clear that it
was not based upon sales figures or sales performance but upon
the assessment as to capacity to adapt to change, including,
according to Mr. Sykes, changing technology and capacity to be
a team player.

The evidence of Mr. Abotomey was that there were 30 redundancies overall in the divisional offices as a consequence of the restructure of the business, however it is clear that as a result there were 6 sales consultants positions in excess of requirements in the Box Hill and Brooklyn regions combined. The majority of alteration to areas was made to those areas previously serviced by sales consultants out of Brooklyn. The majority of redundancies which occurred also occurred in relation to sales consultants engaged to work out of Brooklyn. The applicant, together with one other sales consultant at Box Hill, was selected for redundancy. The person who upon appointment initially serviced the applicant's region whilst she was absent on maternity leave, was allocated one of the new regions in the Melbourne Metropolitan Area. The person transferred from the Customer Service Area was allocated a region which included substantial portions of regional and country Victoria.

All staff present at the workplace were advised of the restructure and the consequent redundancies on 17 June, 1996. The applicant was advised on that day also, upon attending at the workplace at the request of the respondent. Upon attending the meeting the applicant was informed by the then Sales Manager, Mr. Sykes, that her position was redundant owing to restructuring. He then attempted to continue to read from a prepared document advising what her entitlements were and the various counselling and assistance facilities available, however before he had finished the applicant left the room in distress. The applicant left the workplace after briefly visiting the sales area. The following day she contacted Mr. Sykes and established that the person who had been filling her position during her absence on maternity leave had been retained. The evidence of Ms Chisholm, the current sales manager, is that between October and December, 1996, four sales consultant positions became vacant. Each of those positions was filled by either outside or internal appointment.

The respondent contends that it had valid reason based upon the operational requirements of the business for the termination of the employment. The respondent contends that it did not replace the applicant with the person who serviced her area whilst she was on maternity leave. It contends that the applicant's position disappeared as a consequence of the restructure and not as a consequence of the other employee being appointed to the position. The applicant contends that the operational requirements as a result of the restructure did not necessitate the termination of the applicant's employment, either at all or at the time the employment terminated. It contends that the respondent filled a position which otherwise would have been available to the applicant by appointing to that position the person relieving the applicant whilst on maternity leave, a person new to the sales consultants area.

I do not accept that the respondent had valid reason for the termination of the applicant's employment for the following reasons. The applicant was still on maternity leave when her employment was terminated. Whilst having indicated that she would like to return to work earlier there was no obligation on the respondent's behalf to agree to an early return to work. Further it was unpaid maternity leave, the entitlement to which had accrued some time prior and was continuing. The respondent in terminating the employment, terminated also the maternity leave without agreement from the applicant. It terminated the employment at a point in time when having regard to the ongoing maternity leave, there was no 'operational' requirement to do so.

Mr. Abotomey, the General Manager of the Division, conceded that whilst the applicant was on maternity leave, the applicant's position had been "filled" and was allocated a territory under the new restructured system. I do not accept that it was an operational requirement that the applicant's employment be terminated in circumstances where a sales region, which could have been allocated to the applicant, was allocated to an employee whom it had been anticipated would return to her previous duties unless an additional position became available in the sales area.

Mr. Abotomey's evidence was that the respondent selected the applicant for redundancy on the basis that she was alleged *"not to be a team player"* and *"there had been some difficulties between herself and the manager"*. I do not accept that there is evidence in these proceedings to support the contention that the applicant was not a *"team player"*. Mr. Sykes, the Applicant's supervisor and Sales Manager, was equivocal as to his evidence in relation to this aspect of the applicant's performance. This is particularly so in relation to alleged difficulties between the applicant and another staff member. In this regard the applicant's evidence as to those difficulties and lack of co-operation was not refuted. Further her evidence is that the difficulties became extreme in the last few months of her attendance at work prior to maternity leave and there was a reluctance on the part of management to deal with the issue in view of her impending departure on leave. I accept the applicant's evidence in this regard. Her salary review appraisals confirm that in the most recent review she was assessed at a performance level well in excess of other employees who were retained. As to the allegation of difficulties between the applicant and her manager, I am not satisfied that these were matters which had arisen from the applicant's conduct, nor were they difficulties which had impacted upon the applicant's work performance or the workplace functioning. In particular, it was alleged that the applicant in the last week of work prior to going on maternity leave had refused to service clients in her area. The applicant's evidence in this regard was that she had expressed concern that there be consistency of personnel in servicing her clients and that she was reluctant to pursue new orders when she would not be around to follow through. She saw this as damaging to the reputation of the respondent. The applicant also advised that she was unwell in that latter period and that her doctors advice was to finish work.. This was later confirmed by a Doctors Certificate. This was the only matter relied upon by the respondent as supporting the contention that the applicant was unwilling to perform her duties or that there were difficulties between her and the manager. I accept the applicant's evidence in relation to this incident. The applicant's conduct was directed to the interests of the clients of the respondent and did not constitute conduct which would justify any criticism or fault. Whilst I am satisfied that these matters did constitute the taking into account of performance related matters in selecting the applicant for redundancy, I am not satisfied that these unsubstantiated matters were valid to be taken into account in objectively or fairly applying the 'team work' and 'adaptability criteria' that the respondent contends was applied.

The applicant, by operation of *Schedule 14 of the Act*, had a Statutory entitlement to Maternity Leave. She also by that Act had an entitlement to return to work at the cessation of that leave in circumstances where the work which she was performing was

continuing to be performed or to another position. This is not a
situation where the business had closed or ceased entirely to
operate in respect of the applicant's functions. The alterations
which occurred to the zones or sales regions in the metropolitan
area resulted in there still being work performed on a large scale.
The restructure of the manner in which that work was performed
does not enable the respondent to avoid its obligations in respect
of maternity leave and consequent return to work. It is apparent
from the scheme of the legislation that a fundamental element of
the entitlement to maternity leave is the entitlement to return to
work at the expiration of that leave. This is expressed in *Clause
12(2) and (3) of Schedule 14*. No recognition or attempt to
accommodate this obligation was made by the respondent and no
consideration was given to the particular entitlements and
circumstances of the applicant, in that she was absent on
maternity leave. According to Mr. Sykes, all employees were
treated equally and no regard was had for the applicant being on
maternity leave. This failure to have any regard to the applicant's
entitlements under the statute denied her a benefit of protection
provided for by the statute and proper to be taken into account in
the circumstances.

Further, I am not satisfied that the criteria of selection was either
objective or methodically applied. I do not accept the evidence
that the applicant was deemed unsuitable for any of the areas
available. The applicant was particularly well qualified for any of
the metropolitan areas designated. She was one of the
respondent's top sales people. Mr. Sykes, save for the examples
discussed earlier, was unable to identify any objective basis upon
which the applicant had not been selected for a region. It was put
to him by Ms. Richards, counsel for the applicant, that the
selection was based upon a desire to immediately implement the

alterations to the sales areas and that as the applicant would be on leave until January 1997, it was seen as inconvenient to allocate her a sales territory. Mr. Sykes denied that this was so, however he conceded that the respondent was anxious to implement its new arrangements and minimise disruption to clients. In the absence of an explanation as to why the maternity leave period was not allowed to run to its natural conclusion and having regard to the lack of objective criteria applied to the selection of the applicant for redundancy, I am not satisfied that the absence of the applicant on maternity leave was not part of the reason for the termination of her employment. Consequently I am not satisfied that the termination of her employment was not for reasons connected with her sex or parental responsibilities or maternity leave absence, matters prohibited by s170DF(1)(f) and s170DF(1)(g).

Shortly after the applicant's employment had terminated, but before the period of her maternity leave would have expired, the respondent hired additional sales consultants. The evidence of Ms Chisholm, the present Sales Manager, is that four consultants resigned in the period October, 1996 to January, 1997. No offer was made to the applicant of such a position. The operational requirement relied upon by the respondent would not have resulted in the termination of the applicant's employment, if the period of the leave had been allowed to run and the applicant had been allowed to return to work either earlier than or at the conclusion of her maternity leave.

In opening and in the evidence it was put on behalf of the respondent, that work performance and conduct issues did not form any part of the reason for the selection of the applicant for redundancy. I do not accept that this was so. The applicant was selected according to a process of judging her capabilities as a team player and her relations with her manager. These matters were clearly the subject of some criticism. It was the negative view of her capabilities, held by Mr. Sykes that was the reason why she was selected for redundancy. I am satisfied that the applicant was entitled to be informed of these matters by which she was being judged as less capable than other employees. She was also entitled to the opportunity to address the criticisms of her. The applicant was given no opportunity to be heard in relation to either of these matters.

Further, the selection was made in a circumstance where a recommendation was made by a supervisor, Mr. Sykes, the person who raised the issues about her performance, yet the decision of confirming the selection left to persons who had no knowledge of the applicant's performance or conduct vis a vis other employees. The ultimate decision maker, Mr. Abotomey had not met the applicant prior to these proceedings, as he commenced his duties as General Manager after the applicant went on Maternity leave. This is another aspect of the selection of the applicant which identifies the severe disadvantage which she suffered in the selection process as a consequence of being absent from the workplace on maternity leave. She was not present to be able to prove her capacity and performance qualities and she was not given any opportunity to speak to those matters raised against her in this regard.

Consequently there has been a failure to comply with the obligations arising under s170DC of the Act. I am also satisfied that the failure to have regard to these obligations, or the disadvantage under which the applicant suffered, in implementing the redundancy constituted the termination of the employment as unsound or capricious and thus not for valid reason.

For the reasons set out above I find that the respondent did not have valid reason for the termination of the applicant's employment. There has been a contravention of s170DE(1) of the Act. I am not satisfied that the respondent did not have as part of its reason for the termination of the applicant's employment, her parental responsibilities and her absence on authorised maternity leave. There has been a contravention of s170DF(1)(f) and s170DF(1)(g) of the Act. I find also that the respondent failed to accord the applicant an opportunity to be heard in relation to allegations as to her conduct and work performance, being matters which were taken into account in selecting the applicant for redundancy. There has been a contravention of s170DC of the Act. I turn now to consider the question of remedy.

Remedy

As to damage, the respondent contends that there is no compensable damage because the applicant would not have been earning for the period she was on maternity leave and that she was paid a substantial redundancy payment. I do not accept this contention. The purpose of maternity leave is to preserve aspects of benefit in ongoing employment such as seniority, reputation, and career prospects. It is also to provide for return to employment in circumstances where being otherwise on the employment market, may place a new mother at a substantial disadvantage. Those matters are aspects of the damage to the applicant which are ongoing, and not remedied by the payment of a redundancy payment on the same terms as paid to others not suffering from the employment disadvantages and disabilities consequent upon having a young child. One example of this disadvantage arises from the difficulties attendant upon obtaining adequate child care services. The applicant had obtained a place in a child care centre for the period after the expiration of her maternity leave. She had also attempted to obtain a place earlier, in anticipation of returning to work earlier than scheduled. As a consequence of losing her job, and being uncertain of future employment, she was unable to maintain her long standing booking at an adequate child care facility. The applicant faces now the uncertainty of the employment market and the added difficulty of arranging for satisfactory, safe and cost effective child care services. It is obvious that these are the very matters that the provision of maternity leave are designed to address. By enabling a certainty in the period of absence from and return to work, the parent is able to effectively plan for future employment return.

One other aspect is the availability and capacity to look for alternative employment, in circumstances where one is also the attendant carer of a new baby. All of the other employees who were made redundant obtained other positions within days or weeks of the redundancy. This is because they were in a position to make application for such positions and present on a day to day basis at the workplace, enabling them to focus their time and energies on the issues arising. That the Applicant was not available, nor able to pursue her career interests at that time, is a matter arising in my view as a direct consequence of her parental responsibilities and consequent absence on maternity leave and not as a consequence of any failure on her part to mitigate or attempt to mitigate her loss. In this regard I distinguish the applicant's position from the circumstances in *Bechara v Harrison Healey &Co* <u>(1996) 65 IR 382.</u> In that case the applicant had a clear and unequivocal opportunity to return to the former employment, with none of the difficulties which arose for the applicant in this proceeding. No such opportunity was accorded to the applicant in these proceedings.

The applicant's evidence was that as a result of the termination of her employment and its timing, she had suffered a serious loss of self esteem and confidence. She also expressed an ongoing anxiety and difficulty in resolving the issues arising from the incident. For these difficulties she is seeking professional assistance. I accept the applicant's evidence that as a result of the respondent's conduct and the difficulties set out above she felt it was necessary for her to reassess her future career options. I accept that this reassessment was brought about directly as a consequence of the respondent's conduct and could not be assumed to have arisen, but for that conduct. It is apparent from the demeanour and evidence of the applicant that she is struggling to resolve the issues that have arisen as a result of the termination of her employment. The applicant does not seek reinstatement to the employment. In view of the circumstances of the termination and the numerous matters set out above, I accept that such an order would be impracticable. I am satisfied that in all of the circumstances the applicant is entitled to a remedy and that remedy ought be in compensation.

The applicant is entitled to compensation. The compensation awarded arises from my assessment of the ongoing financial loss to the applicant as a consequence of the respondent's conduct. The applicant received a redundancy payment from the respondent. When she went on unpaid maternity leave, the applicant was earning a gross amount of $755.00 per week. She had indicated a desire to return to work earlier than January, 1997, and I am satisfied that but for the decision of the respondent to terminate her employment, the applicant would have returned to work in either June or July, 1996. At that time she would return on the same salary as previously earned. At the time of the hearing of this matter the applicant had not obtained alternative employment. I accept that the applicant's losses were ongoing to at least the date of the trial. It is uncertain when she will be in a position to re-establish herself in full time employment. I accept that the redundancy payment in part is attributable to the period of time after the date of the employment terminated. Having regard to the likely early return to work, that period runs beyond that time and some account ought be made for the ongoing loss suffered by the applicant.

It is clear in this proceeding that a redundancy payment was made. This is a matter to be taken into account in determining the compensable loss of the applicant. I accept the submission of Ms. Richards as to the components of the redundancy payment made to the applicant. I am satisfied that the redundancy payment included a component attributable to pro-rata long service leave. This is the sum of $5,331.49. The rest of the payment is made up in accordance with a formula of 3 weeks pay for each year of service, amounting to a sum of $15,859.20. There was no evidence in the proceedings to the contrary in terms of the manner of calculating the entitlement. It is clear from the authorities as to the purpose and components of redundancy payments (see in this regard *Termination, Change &*

Redundancy Case [1984] AILR 256) that only part of that redundancy payment is attributable to the ongoing losses suffered in terms of income. A significant component of any redundancy benefit is attributable to loss of career prospects, future accrued leave entitlements, pay increases, seniority, superannuation accruals, sick leave accruals, and other benefits not necessarily payable as cash, such as private use of motor vehicles.

In the particular circumstances of the applicant I am satisfied that the losses exceed those which may have been compensated by the redundancy payment. One example of this additional loss is that is apparent that the applicant, unlike all other sales representatives made redundant on the same day, did not obtain employment shortly thereafter. In the circumstances I am satisfied that it appropriate in awarding compensation, to account for half of the redundancy payment when compensating the loss, as this can reasonably be attributable as a payment to compensate for future lost income. This is the amount of $7,929.60. The 4 weeks payment in lieu of notice, the statutory entitlement paid should also be deducted from any compensation order. It is not relevant to take into account that amount which I have attributed to a Long Service Leave component, nor consequently, to additionally compensate for that loss in any order for compensation.

I am satisfied that the applicant is entitled to compensation equivalent to 6 months remuneration, on account of the period between July, 1996 and mid January, 1997. That is an amount of $18,124.80. However, that amount is to be reduced by the sum of

$10,950.40 on account of the matters set out above. The order for compensation will be in the sum of $7,174.40. This is a gross amount and payable as such.

I certify that the preceding fourteen (14) pages

are a true copy of the reasons for decision of

Judicial Registrar Parkinson.

Associate :

Dated : 2 May 1997

APPEARANCES

Counsel appearing for the applicant : Ms. M. Richards

Solicitors for the applicant : Slater & Gordon

Counsel appearing for the respondent : Mr. S. Wood

Solicitors for the respondent : Arthur Robertson & Hedderwicks

Date of hearing : 19 & 20 February 1997.

Chapter 11

What the hell is wrong with me?

When the court case was done and dusted, I felt the need to prove to myself that I could 'just get on with it'. I didn't celebrate that I had won my case, as everyone I knew, whether family or friends, all seemed to think I was crazy to have gone through with my unfair dismissal case. But I was one of those people who wasn't going to just roll over and take it anymore as I had been treated badly by employers in the past, and I didn't want Amcor to get away with what they had done to me. If everyone was like that, then all the arsehole bosses in this world (sadly, there are a lot of them) would get away with it. Proving a company has done something wrong is hard, but I don't think they should be left unaccountable.

I got the proof that Amcor had treated me badly, but afterwards I did have mixed emotions about whether it had been worth it, due to what other people thought. I didn't talk about it much after the court case was over and the decision had been made; I just wanted to put it all behind me and get another job as money was getting tight.

After a couple of months, I ended up getting a job back in sales. I put my son into childcare and tried to move forward. I was only in the job for about a year and then decided to leave as my heart just wasn't in it. I had proved to them I was good in sales as I had renegotiated some large contracts for the company and saved them a lot of money, but I wondered if I was trying to prove something to myself, or was it trying to prove to others that I could dust myself off and move on from the past year? Thinking back, I know it was about proving to others more than myself. Why is it that we have to put on a show for other people when it really shouldn't matter what they think?

Unfortunately, I think we are all guilty of doing this.

I felt that I was missing too much time with my son, so I decided to give up my job and be a full-time mum, something that previously I didn't think I would do. The fact was, most of my money was going into childcare fees and it was hardly worth working.

Not much has changed when it comes to childcare fees; they are out of control. It is like sending your child to an expensive private school. Unlike today, where you can get childcare subsidies, I didn't have that privilege. But as much as subsidies are available today, it can still be difficult to get your child into good quality care. A lot of mums just want to work part-time when they have children, but it is just not worth it if they have to pay childcare costs.

When it comes to being a full-time working mum, having to juggle work and raising children is bloody hard work, and if you have the opportunity to not work, why the hell not be a full-time mum for a while? I admire women who have great careers as I know they would have worked hard to get where they are. Women are told, 'We can have it all, now,' but the reality is there is a high cost.

I have seen women who work full-time try to be superwoman and it's not easy. I thought I could be, but I felt that I was missing too much. Only having the weekends to really spend time with my child because I was flat-out working, coming home each night to do mealtime, bath time and then getting baby to bed was too much. By the time I had done all of that I just collapsed. Then I had to do it all again the next day; it was a bit like Groundhog Day.

When the weekend came, I would have liked a bit of time to myself, but when you have children it's hard to find that time. That is where superwoman comes into play. Women can be the worst at judging other mothers if they can't get to a playgroup or you've purchased a cake from the supermarket for morning tea instead of baking one, or you're just running late. You can get judged even if you are a full-time mum, but when you're working full-time you seem to get judged even harder.

Brené Brown, in her book *I thought it was just me (but it isn't)*, writes about feeling inadequate and dealing with shame, judgement, criticism and blame by seeking safety in pretending and perfection. I look back now and see that is exactly what I was doing; a bloody fantastic job of making everyone think I was fine when in fact I was falling apart. What I refer to as 'faking it'.

So, I quit my job, which I was finding pretty boring anyway. It shitted me that I was working with a lot of men again, and dealing with the sexism was eye-rolling. For the next three years I was a full-time mum. I look back and remember the time I spent with my little boy as a wonderful experience. I will never regret my decision because children grow up quickly and before you know it you wonder where the time went.

My fondest memories from that time are playing in a park near to our house as it had a large ship where you could pretend to play pirates, plus a long slide that my son absolutely loved. Children are so innocent and totally reliant on you plus the unconditional love they show you. I probably needed that time not to work, and all I had to think about was looking after my boy.

When my son started kindergarten, I got a part-time job at a travel company. I felt like I was starting all over again at the age of thirty-six as the first job I had was at a travel company, and that hadn't ended well. This was a low-paying job, *very* low, but I wanted to get back into the workforce and didn't want to take on a high-pressure sales job. The position was doing reception work, meeting and greeting plus answering the phone.

The job was pretty boring, but it helped me get back into the swing of working. Sadly, there was a lot of bitching, backstabbing and political bullshit that went with it. I had absolutely no patience for it. Being on reception, I had people from the office talking to me about (or should I say, 'bitching about') someone else. I used to think I should be getting paid a lot more for this job as I felt like a psychologist, not a menially paid receptionist. I listened, was sympathetic and tried hard not to get involved.

Once my son started school, and I was able to get after-school care, I left the travel company and started doing temporary office work. It was mainly reception work, even though I was capable of a lot more, but I was good at reception and many businesses requested me back, so I got regular temporary assignments. I worked for a lot of different companies and saw how they operated. I lost count of how many companies I worked for: large corporations, medium-sized companies plus small businesses. Sadly, the one thing that became obvious was that most of them were the same when it came to bullying, bitching, backstabbing, discrimination and men holding most of the senior management positions.

Taking on temporary work that lasted anywhere from one week to two months and then moving on was good in that I didn't get dragged into any corporate political bullshit, and that suited me down to the ground. The jobs tended to be one's people didn't want to do, or I filled in as a receptionist when the permanent person went on holiday. Lots of people see being a receptionist as a menial job and, as far as I am concerned, it is the most undervalued job in any company and usually one of the lowest paying, plus it is predominantly women who do it.

Let's put a receptionist's job in perspective:

- You have to be friendly and greet everyone that comes through the door with a smile.

- You have to be well presented and groomed.

- You have to have an excellent phone manner and know where and how to transfer calls.

- You have to juggle incoming and internal calls.

- You have to coordinate pickups and deliveries.

- You have to be the person who knows where everyone is in the building, and when, where and what they do.

- You have to screen calls and pretend that the person they need to speak to isn't there when they really are.

- Oh, and you have to be a mind reader.

Most importantly, you are the face of the company. You are the first person who takes the call and usually the one who cops the brunt of a dissatisfied customer or client. Sadly, this job is one of the lowest paying in the whole company, yet you are the face of the company and are the first impression people get about a business.

There are lots of other tasks added to the job depending on who you work for, and you have to juggle those as well as being the go-to person when it comes to someone wanting to vent their anger about someone else in the office, so we could add psychologist to the list.

The one thing I learnt quickly was who the workers were in the office and who were the slackers. Receptionists redirect all the calls so you know who is busy and who spends most of their time at the water station talking shit and you can never find them. Sadly, they seem to be the ones who keep their jobs as they are great at sucking up to the boss. As much as doing this type of work fitted in with my life at the time, I did want to get back into a good sales job again and do what I did best. I was a good communicator and good in sales and I didn't want to be in temporary jobs for the rest of my life.

Looking for another sales job was daunting and applying for jobs and going for interviews wasn't easy. I had lost a lot of my confidence and, more importantly, trust that a company would do the right thing by me. I had been burnt badly by Amcor and crawling my way back was not going to be easy.

I still didn't want to work full-time as I wanted to have time to fit everything in when it came to my son, having the house in order, cooking, shopping and all the other things that go with family life. It's still hard even with a part-time job, but when you work full-time it's just crazy. I admire single mothers as they have to do it all, although in a lot of cases even if you do have a partner, it is still the woman who does the majority of the chores around the house.

I ended up getting a job with a furniture importer, and I was back on the road visiting clients again. It was a small company with about ten staff members and two people on the road selling. The other man in sales had worked for the company for well over fifteen years and he was not helpful at all. I found out the hard way that I couldn't sell certain furniture items to my clients as that impacted his clients' ability to sell them. When I asked to have a list of items I couldn't sell, he was reluctant to give it to me. I couldn't understand why this was such an issue. When I spoke to the owner of the business about it, he said he would speak to him and get a list.

I continued to see clients and try to work out what I could sell and what I couldn't. Having a list would have made my life easier but I couldn't see that happening in a hurry as the other salesperson simply didn't want to do it. For the next few months, I did well in getting new clients and selling stock. I just avoided selling a lot of items that I knew were popular. Ridiculous, I know, but that is what I was working with.

I finally got a list from the other salesperson, and he had written a note saying, 'Better late than never.' I thought, *What a smart arse!* The list was a scribble at best and really didn't tell me much at all. I then had a meeting with the owner and showed him the list and he knew it wasn't good enough. He said he would speak again to the other salesperson.

I finally realised that the only reason why I couldn't sell a lot of the items was that it would impact the other salesperson's commission. That was it, nothing to do with agreements with clients, it was all bullshit and also to make my life harder. He had run the show in sales on his own for many years and now here was a new person in the mix. He did everything possible to make my job difficult.

The next time I spoke with the owner he was not in a good mood. He was a stern person and most people in the office seemed to fear him, and he was also intimidating. We were discussing sales, which I was doing well with, and the issue of selling various items that I was told I couldn't sell by the other salesperson. He just started yelling at me about why I wasn't selling more coffee tables. I'm thinking, *Because there isn't much margin in them.* Selling lounges was making him a lot of money, not coffee tables.

He continued to yell at me, and I couldn't get a word in. I could feel my tears starting to well up, so I kept looking down. I finally looked up and he could see I was just about to burst into tears, something I tried hard not to do. He just sat there glaring at me and said nothing. We stared at each other for what seemed like an eternity, and then I stood up and walked out of his office. He said nothing as I walked out. I went to the car and took a few deep breaths then drove home to finish my paperwork and finish up for the day.

When I got home and sat at the computer to fill in a few sales reports, I opened up my emails and could see one from the owner of the business. The email was short but to the point; he was sacking me!

All it said was that he no longer required me to work with his business, and could I return all brochures and sample materials to the office as soon as possible. I just sat there looking at this email in complete shock. I thought, *You gutless prick.* How can you sack someone via email!

So, I packed up my work folders and sample books of materials on the lounge, placed them in a box and my husband took them back to the office the next day. I didn't want to look at him ever again.

Here was a man who intimidated his staff, but he didn't have the guts to dismiss me face to face. Tells you a lot about what kind of person he was!

In the following months I had to continue to call the accounts department as I had sales commission money owing to me. A considerable amount that I was *not* going to let the owner get away with not paying me. Obviously, he would have had to sign off on these payments and he would have seen that I'd been doing exceptionally well selling his furniture. I hoped that his decision to sack me via email was all about him having a hissy fit and later regretting it, but at the end of the day, it was his loss. He was stuck with a salesperson who wasn't really looking after the company's interests, only his own regarding his commission cheque.

A couple of years later I looked the company up to see if it was still operating, and I found that it had closed, belly up as they say.

Losing a job again was hard to swallow, and I naturally wondered if it was me. What was wrong with me? My confidence felt more shattered, and I ended up going back to temporary work. The job agency loved me and many companies requested me. The agency always got great reports about my performance, so that made me feel better about myself. But deep down I really thought something was wrong with me.

Chapter 12

Becoming an expert

I was reluctant to take on another permanent job as I was afraid of losing another one. When you lose a job, embarrassment, shame, worthlessness, self-pity and depression are all part of the fallout, and this was something I continued to struggle with. I tried to be strong and 'move on' but the cracks were well and truly forming. I was falling into a black hole and didn't notice as I was numbing the pain with alcohol and dope. I enjoyed a good joint, but it was mainly at parties, which were few and far between as I had a child. I still functioned well, and everything looked fine to others on the outside but inside my head was different.

While working for a flavouring company on a temporary assignment, I was offered the job permanently. I was reluctant at first, but I decided it would be nice to be in a steady job for a while, so I accepted. It was a receptionist job, which also included putting all the sales orders into the computer. The sales manager was great, everyone loved him as he was easy to get along with. After a couple of months, he could see that having me doing reception was a bit of a waste of my experience, so they hired another receptionist and I was put in charge of all orders and dealing with customers over the phone, coordinating their deliveries. Everything was going well, and I was gaining a good rapport with the customers.

The business also had an office manager who had worked for the company for well over ten years. He was a quirky man, but I got along fairly well with him. I really had little to do with him as I reported to the sales manager. One week I noticed that the office manager wasn't there and wondered if he was sick. When I asked the general manager's PA (who knew everything that was going on) if he was sick, she told me that he'd been told to go on leave. Apparently, he'd lost his shit with the company cleaners, and they'd made a formal complaint against him. The rumour was that he had split with his partner and was in a bad space.

During this time, the sales manager resigned. Everyone was shattered as he was such a great manager, but he'd been offered a job he couldn't refuse as the money was too good. Just before he left, he told me a bit more about the office manager and that his job was on tenterhooks. I felt for him as I knew what it was like to lose a job, and if he had lost his partner then losing his job would be a massive thing to deal with. On his return, I did my best to get along with him and just do my job.

A new sales manager was hired, and he was a lovely man. We got along well, he was learning the business and had figured out that changes needed to be made. Not long after he started, the office manager came back to work, and you could tell he was not a happy camper. I just kept my distance as much as I could but when it came to computer issues, he was the one you had to speak to.

One day I went to his office to talk about some of the computer problems we were having with placing orders into the system. Standing in the doorway of his office, asking if he had time to discuss it, he looked up at me angrily and threw his pen down on the desk. I took a step back and just looked a bit startled. The PA to the general manager was in the hallway at the time and she saw the look on my face. She gave me a look as if to say, 'What the hell is going on?' I just walked away from his office and went back to my desk. Later that day, the PA came up to me and said, 'What happened with the office manager?' I told her, 'I just went to discuss with him about the computers and he cracked the shits, threw his pen down and glared at me.' She then went on to tell me he had lost his shit with the cleaners and that's why he was told to take time off. I didn't let on that I already knew that had happened.

About a week later, the office manager said he wanted to have a meeting with me. I assumed it was about the computers. Well, I was wrong; he went on about how I wasn't doing my job properly but couldn't come up with any specifics. I thought this was strange as I didn't report his actions to anyone but was now thinking I should have. I knew immediately that this was a power play by him, so I asked him to give specific incidents and he couldn't. Walking out of the meeting, I remember thinking, *Fucking hell, I'm dealing with a very angry person*. The next day I had a meeting with my sales manager, and he said that he would sort it all out. For the next few days, I just got on with my job and kept my distance from the office manager.

The following week I had another meeting with the sales manager and the accounts manager. Both had started their jobs after me so we were all newbies with the company. They both sat opposite me in the boardroom, looking solemn. I knew something was up; I could feel it in my bones. They informed me that they were letting me go. Yes, I was being sacked once again.

I was one week out from my six-month trial period. Not once had they spoken to me about my job performance. The only person who I did have these discussions with, and who loved my work, was the sales manager who had left. He was the one who knew I was being wasted on the reception desk and moved me into the customer service role. I knew the office manager had everything to do with this and that he just wanted me out of the way. He considered me a threat, but the reality was I didn't want his job at all. I liked dealing with clients; being an office manager didn't interest me.

The accounts manager left the boardroom looking a bit rattled as he'd obviously been asked there as a witness. The sales manager didn't have much to say. I went to my desk to gather my things and he asked me to come into his office. That is when I started to cry and said, 'What the hell is wrong with me?' He was sympathetic and said I could stay in his office as long as I liked. After about ten minutes I got up and said, 'Well, I'd better pack up my stuff and get the hell out of here.' He said he was sorry about what was happening, but it was out of his hands. I really didn't know what he was meaning by this as he was my direct boss and had just sacked me!

I went to my desk, got my things and walked out of the building without saying anything to anyone. The sales manager followed me out and gave me a big hug outside the building where nobody could see us, and he wished me good luck. I said to him, 'Maybe I should be wishing you good luck working for this company.' He said, 'I think you might be right.' We said our goodbyes and I drove home.

I went through the bottle shop on the way home and got hammered that night.

I really did think that something was wrong with me. Why was I becoming an expert at losing jobs?

I decided to get in contact with the sales manager that had left the company. As I had to look for yet another job, I wanted to know if he could be a referee for me. When I told him what had happened, he was totally shocked. He knew straight away that the office manager was behind it and that the general manager was weak when it came to making decisions. He admitted that one of the main reasons he'd left was because he couldn't make changes as the general manager was hopeless. He had no problem at all being a referee for me as he thought I was wonderful at my job and thought it was ridiculous I'd been let go.

I felt a bit better knowing that he would be a referee for me and that losing my job was all about getting me out of the way because the office manager saw me as a threat. But here I was, I had lost another job.

The job agency I'd worked for, and also the one who got me the gig at the flavouring company, were also shocked by what had happened. They continued to give me other assignments, but now my faith in any company was shattered. I had no trust at all, my depression was getting worse and so was my drinking.

Chapter 13

Male-dominated industries

I continued to work in temporary jobs for a while, and then I stumbled upon a part-time job with a magazine producer. It was a magazine about families and childcare. It was a small company, and the people were lovely to work with. Finally, I thought I had found a job I liked. It consisted of various tasks in sales and getting the office systems in order as it was a bit of a shambles. They loved me and all was good in the world, and then the Global Financial Crisis hit in 2008 and the company sank. It was hit hard by losing advertisers, and four of us were laid off.

I was devastated.

The one good thing that came out of it was that it had nothing to do with me, but I was still back on the job scrapheap along with a lot of other people who lost their jobs at the time.

Thankfully, it didn't take long before I got a gig with an employment agency who were wanting a team of salespeople in Melbourne to look after the electrical companies that supplied the wiring in building projects. A team of about ten women were employed from Melbourne and Sydney, and we all had to do a training session with the main supplier in Sydney. It was all paid for – flights, accommodation and food – and we spent three days in training. It was a great group of women, and we actually had a lot of fun. We were all given areas we had to look after and had to call on electrical businesses that supplied cables to various building contractors. None of them had dealt with women before in the industry, and all the ladies contracted to do the job were having issues dealing with aggressive and rude men who didn't want to deal with women.

We had boobs so therefore we had no brains!

Many of the women left within a couple of months as they couldn't handle the despicable way they were being treated by some of the electrical suppliers. I had thoughts of bailing too, but I hung in there as I had dealt with a lot of men in the past and had gotten used to shrugging off a lot of the sexist comments.

One of my customers was one of the rudest men I have ever met. He was so arrogant and rude to me it's a wonder I didn't slap his face. Every time I went to see him, he would make me wait forever. He made it so obvious that he hated dealing with me because I was a woman. The industry hadn't had females selling to these electrical dealers before, and I wasn't the only woman dealing with clients that disliked having female sales representatives. Unfortunately, he was a major supplier in the Melbourne area.

All the women had to report to the agency about how things were going, and all of them said how hard it was to deal with the men in the industry. The woman from the employment agency who'd interviewed us had left due to being pregnant and she'd been replaced by a man. He had never met any of us and was trying to get a grip on what was going on and why the women were leaving.

We had weekly phone discussions with him and kept him updated on sales so he could report back to the main supplier. Then one day he called me all chatty and asked how I was going. But I got this horrible feeling the conversation was going somewhere. He informed me that a complaint had been made against me and they were letting me go. When I asked who had made the complaint, he wouldn't tell me or what the complaint was, and that was that. This was all done over the phone from a person I'd never met.

Well, at least it wasn't an email this time!

Speaking with one of the other women who worked in the Melbourne area, who I got along well with, she had been told that the 'arsehole' that worked with the large supplier in Melbourne had refused to deal with me. Due to the fact he was one of Melbourne's largest suppliers, the company thought it was best that they just let me go.

I did write an email to most of the senior managers at the electrical company and express my disappointment at how my dismissal was handled. The email was also sent to the general manager, who actually called me, which took me by complete surprise. He told me he was disappointed in what had happened and that he would talk to the employment agency about it. After a couple of days, I found out from one of the other women also contracted to work for the electrical company that they'd been told that nobody was to talk to me about what'd happened and it was never to be raised again.

The fact was, the electrical company wanted to distance itself from my dismissal in case I lodged a claim for unfair dismissal, which I was more than justified in doing. I really didn't want to go down that path again and frankly I didn't want to work with the agency or the electrical company again either. The electrical company didn't sack me, the agency did, and therefore my claim for unfair dismissal would have been made against them. The electrical company didn't want to involve themselves in what had occurred. Subsequently, I never heard back from the general manager of the electrical company. I later found out that he was told by the company's legal department not to contact me again for fear of being dragged into a legal situation involving the employment agency.

Once again, on the job scrapheap, and to me it was just because a man couldn't deal with a woman.

My downward spiral continued, and my self-worth was crushed. I never wanted to work for another company ever again.

Chapter 14

Covering up the pain

As I was a good cook, I decided to start my own business. Working for myself seemed to be the only answer as I couldn't face losing another job and being sacked again. I couldn't go through the pain again. It's horrible to lose a job no matter what the circumstances are, but when you're being sacked and you really can't understand why, it is a hard pill to swallow.

The fact was, I was embarrassed about losing these jobs, and the impact was bigger than I ever realised. People would tell me to 'dust yourself off and get back on the bike', 'move on' or 'just get over it'. Most of these people had no idea what it felt like to lose a job and how much it crushed you. I was starting to lose count of how many jobs I had lost and how many times I'd had to 'dust myself off' and 'move on'.

Adding to this, my marriage was crumbling. I really wanted to leave and start my life over again, from the beginning, but you can't do that, you can't go back, you can only move forward. So, forward I went and started up my own business being a personal cook for people who didn't have the time to cook and who relied on takeaway. They wanted to eat better and have healthy home-cooked meals.

I set up a website and did some advertising, and I got my first gig working for a family of five. Mum, Dad and three boys. The father owned a large health-food business and they were wealthy people. They had a full-time maid, and the father wanted his boys to eat better, plus he wanted to as well. The company he owned was into health products so he really needed to walk the talk. I worked with this family for about a year. I also got gigs with others including a well-known Australian singer, a writer for a popular TV show and a couple of elderly men whose wives had passed away and they hated meals on wheels.

So, I was kept busy; I had only myself to answer to and I wasn't about to sack myself.

It was hard work, but I liked it because I had no managers to deal with. I got along with all my customers, and they loved my food, but I was not in a good place. I covered up my pain with drinking and smoking. I still functioned well, so it wasn't like I was waking up and wanting to have a drink; I only did it when I got home from work. I *never* smoked in front of my son.

The fact was that I was numbing the pain. I would drink a bottle of wine or more every night and smoke marijuana on top of that. I look back and wonder how I functioned, but I did. I dropped my son off at school, went to work, came home and cooked for the family. I also kept the house clean and did all the shopping and everything ran smoothly. When my husband got home, dinner was almost always on the table, and if anyone happened to drop over and visit, everything looked fine.

I was doing a *fantastic* job of faking it.

I was keeping up appearances in the face of what I believed was expected of me. I think the workplace is somewhere people fake it all the time. Whether it is about how much work they do, or if they don't like someone, if they hate the boss or hate their job. Let's face it, if you didn't have to work for someone else, why would you? If you won millions of dollars in Tattslotto, you would probably be out of the workplace in a flash. Yes, some people like their jobs and might stay because it has become their life, and if that makes them happy then keep working. But most people wouldn't hesitate to leave if they won lots of money. As for me, you wouldn't see me for the dust when driving out of the carpark.

Some people define themselves by the work they do and how much money they make, but are they happy? Are they really doing what they want to do or just doing what they have to do to get by? Are they just keeping up with the Joneses, with a big house, nice car and luxury holidays and making out they have everything in life that anyone would want? Some maybe, but most are probably up to their eyeballs in debt and are stressing all the time about how to keep up their fake lifestyle.

When I was falling into the black hole, I was working for myself in my own cooking business, and I was gaining more clients. My husband worked full-time and financially we were keeping our heads above water. Yes, we did have a mortgage, but we really didn't have much to pay off as we'd purchased the house when prices were not as out of control as they are now. It was a lovely home, a 1920s weatherboard that we renovated. It was in a nice inner suburb of Melbourne, and it was close to shops and schools. It had a lovely garden and even a picket fence.

From the outside most people thought everything was fine, but behind closed doors I felt like my life was crumbling. I kept trying to convince myself that everything was okay when it was far from it. Drinking and smoking every night was a clear sign that I wasn't happy.

When I look at society today, we really do drink a lot, and it is something that has become accepted too. But why are we drinking? Not only drinking but drug taking as well. It is a big problem, not only in Australia but around the world.

So, like many people I was doing a great job of faking it and letting everyone believe all was good in my world.

Chapter 15

Falling into the black hole

On 14th May 2013, I left my husband of twenty-six years. It is a day that will be burnt into my memory forever.

I don't think our marriage was very different from many long-term relationships, where things had become a bit like Groundhog Day. I won't deny that my mental health was well and truly on the decline, and I felt that the only way I could get better was to leave.

With the accumulation of all that had happened, I knew I had to sort myself out.

My husband and I had been happy for many years, but I knew we had grown apart. I can't even express how miserable I had become. I stayed for so long because I was trying to keep it all together for our son, plus a huge part of me thought this was just how life was. You got married, bought a house, had children, got old and retired sitting on the front veranda in your rocking chairs.

Life is not that simple.

We only ever had one child – whom I adore more than anything – and leaving my son behind crushed my heart. I will never forget sitting with him on the front porch, and he was sobbing when I told him I was moving out. I almost said that I wouldn't go, but in my heart of hearts I knew it was the best thing for me. Selfish is something many people would say I was. People are so quick to judge someone else's actions without knowing the full story.

I had decided to not take my son with me because I didn't want his routine to change. He was seventeen at the time and heading into his last year of secondary college. I tried to stay until he had finished school, but I knew I couldn't as thoughts of taking my own life had become constant. I had fallen into the black hole of depression so badly that digging my way out was going to be hard. I felt that because I was the one who wasn't happy in the marriage, I should be the one to leave.

My husband and I had spoken on many occasions about our marriage but nothing really changed, and I don't think he really knew how unhappy I had become, even though it was spoken about.

Sometimes I would be at home on my own and think about how I could take my life: jumping in front of a train, but then I'd think about how this would impact the train driver; maybe I would hang myself or gas myself in the car while it was parked in the garage, but then the possibility of my son being the one to find me was too horrendous.

I really didn't have enough money to move out, so I decided to ask my sister for some money. She was financially stable. I met up with her for lunch; she had no idea what she was about to be told.

I remember being at the café and we were just waffling on. I was reluctant to tackle the conversation about money while in the café in case I broke down and other people stared at me. But I also felt desperate at the prospect of getting on with my life and finally feeling good about myself and being happy again, although the reality was that I still had a long way to go before I could feel that way.

When we got back to my sister's house and we were still sitting in her car, I completely lost it and started crying to the point where I could hardly get my words out. I finally told her I wanted to leave my husband and asked if she could help me with some money so I could move into a small apartment near my son's school.

She admitted that she could see I wasn't happy over the years, but sadly she never asked me if I was okay. Not that different to most people who can see that something is wrong but don't ask due to not wanting to get involved or feeling that they are sticking their nose in.

She helped me and I managed to get a small apartment, but it was in the building from hell. It had so many issues with poor ventilation, and I almost fell in the shower because the tiles were so slippery. They were actually wall tiles on the floor so that made them slimy. I then had to have a man come and remove the tiles, which created dust all over the place. The walls were so thin that I could hear what was going on in the apartments next to me, and the smell of some people's cooking made me want to vomit.

I was in a really bad way and shouldn't have been on my own, but I put on a brave face (I was really good at that) and spent my time going to the family home and painting the house we were about to put on the market and sell. I would get up and go to the house, paint all day, and when my son came home from school, I would get him something to eat and ask about his day, then I would leave before my husband got home. When I was painting during the day I would often be crying and painting at the same time as I had put a lot of hard work into making the family home look beautiful, and many people commented on how lovely our house was. It was breaking my heart at the thought of selling it. I had to keep thinking, 'It's just a house, Linda.'

Due to the poor ventilation in the shitty apartment, I made a complaint to the real estate agent. I found it was a problem in the entire building, plus some apartments had water from balconies above them leaking into their lounge rooms. I told the agent I wanted out and they agreed to break the lease because they knew the issues with the building.

I had only been in the apartment for about four months, but I had to get out as it was only making me worse. My cousin offered me a room to stay in, and I was grateful for her offer. I stayed there for a couple of months, but I felt like I was a burden, even though she was not at the house a lot. I made the decision to move back with my parents. At the age of forty-nine, I was back in the family home I was raised in and sleeping in my old bedroom.

Moving so many times just made me even more depressed, but I pushed forward. Yes, I kept 'dusting myself off', 'picking myself up' and 'moving on'. As most of my things were just in boxes, I just shoved them in the car and moved.

I knew I was running on an empty tank, and all of my focus was on fixing up the house, selling it and buying a little place for myself. I couldn't really 'move on' until I had the money from the house sale to start a new life and finally begin to feel better about myself. My depression was getting worse, and I finally realised I needed more help than just being on anti-depressants.

I got a referral from my doctor to see a psychologist. I had a mental health plan organised by my doctor, which allowed ten subsidised appointments I could attend in twelve months. I only knew about this through my good friend who was dealing with her own issues. My doctor never told me about it, otherwise I would have done it earlier. I really don't understand why she didn't raise this with me, maybe she assumed I had money, I'm not really sure, but it would have been great to know about that sooner.

We sold the house, which broke my heart as I'd invested so much of myself in it. My husband hoped I'd come back when we sold it, but I think the reality of the situation started to sink in.

He wasn't happy with the settlement as it wasn't 50/50. I actually thought it would be, but I was advised by my solicitor that it never splits 50/50 because women are at a financial disadvantage as they earn less than men. That is why most settlements favour the woman. It's not because women are trying to rip men off.

I've heard men bitch about this over the years saying, 'My wife hasn't worked all her life like I have,' or, 'We've gained this wealth together over the years, why should she get more?' These are just a couple of statements I've heard; some I can't repeat.

It is a well-known fact that women earn less money, and a lot of women take time off to have children and raise them. A lot of men forget that it's the woman who maintains the house and looks after the kids, and that is a bloody full-time unpaid job.

My settlement was 60/40. I could have gotten a higher percentage but frankly I wanted it over. I didn't want to have a fight and have the lawyers eat away at our money on legal fees.

Once the settlement was done, I had the money to move out of my parents' home and rent a house near my son's school. I found a pretty crappy house, but it was all I could afford, and I was spiralling into the black hole faster than I could have ever imagined.

My son split his time between my house and his father's, which really wasn't a good thing for him, but we both wanted to show him that we loved him. He wanted to spend time with both of us as well, but it did impact his schooling. I can look at him now, eight years later, and see he has grown into a resilient young man. I have a very good relationship with him, and every time we speak I always say, 'love you', and he does the same.

I lived in that house for a year. It was old and rundown, plus it had little light coming in. It really wasn't a good place for me to be in, but I knew I wouldn't be there forever.

I was still managing to get some cooking gigs, but I largely dipped into my settlement money to pay the rent. While living at that house, I was alone most of the time when my son was staying with his father. I had one friend check in on me, and my sister called on the phone every couple of weeks, but that was it. My depression meant I was at an all-time low and my alcohol diet covered up the pain. My smoking reduced though I did dabble, but I really couldn't afford it, which was a good thing really.

I was losing lots of weight, which was not a bad thing as I needed to lose some, but I rarely ate as I was so stressed from all the moving and feeling alone in my journey. I lost 10kg in one year. I know my parents were worried about me, but I was someone who kept pushing on and trying to keep it together, even though I felt like I was dying inside.

When I did bump into people, they would say I looked great, but if they asked me how I lost the weight I imagined saying, 'I call it the alcohol diet, plenty of booze and no food, it's fantastic, I'll send you the program.' I could just imagine the look on their faces.

It was also at this time when two good friends (or so I thought) pushed me further into the black hole.

Chapter 16

Family, friends and foes

The one thing I have learnt about people over the years is that there are takers and givers. Obviously, the takers are the ones who only think about themselves and have little regard to how other people are. The givers are the ones who have the guts to talk about the bad things in life, discuss it with you and actually care how you are and make the effort to be a true friend, something which is hard to find.

The givers are usually people who have had great challenges to overcome in their lives, and when I mean great, I mean *big*.

Great sadness and coming to terms with it can be a constant struggle, and sometimes you can never get over it but learn to live with it, which is a constant struggle in itself. People who tell you to move on and get over it are people who're unlikely to have ever had to deal with great sadness and hurt, so they have little idea what it is like. I have no doubt that everyone has to deal with sadness and people hurting them during their lifetime, but I mean *great* sadness and hurt, and not everyone has had to deal with that. Some people do live charmed lives and, unfortunately, they are the ones who will usually tell you to move on.

You might have events happen in your life that you do move on from, but then something else comes along and you get knocked down again and again and again. You pick yourself up and dust yourself off, but another rock is hurled your way. Eventually, all those rocks can turn into mountains and are therefore much harder to climb.

The greatest sadness, without a doubt, is the loss of a child; every parent's worst nightmare. I only have one son and I really don't know if I could move on from a loss like that.

My son was only five the first time I left my husband early in our marriage, and I went and stayed with my parents as I really didn't have anywhere else to go. I took my son with me that time, and I lived with them for about three months. They couldn't understand why I'd left and neither did the rest of my family. They must have seen I wasn't happy, but I felt that they all thought I was mad to leave. I was deeply unhappy, and I just couldn't seem to get through to them that my marriage had crumbled. My husband wasn't a bad person, he never hurt me physically and he was a good provider, but something was very lost in our marriage.

As for my friends, they stayed away in droves and didn't want to 'get involved', which I see as just an excuse and a cop out. Ringing someone to ask if you are okay is not getting involved as far as I'm concerned, it's just showing you care. I was told once that most people are so busy with their own lives that they don't have the time to deal with other people's problems.

I understand that we all have things going on in our lives, but a simple phone call can sometimes make all the difference in the world, and it doesn't mean you're getting involved. I remember feeling alone and that I was a bad person for leaving my husband, so I ended up going back to him and trying to work things through.

I can look back now and see why people thought I was mad for leaving as everything looked fine to friends and family on the outside. Behind closed doors people didn't see my sadness as I wasn't good at showing that. I generally come across as a strong person who loves to laugh and enjoys good company, but I also know I'm good at putting up a front.

So, for the next twelve years I stayed in the marriage, but my downward spiral continued, and I never really talked to anyone about how bad I really felt. I did try to talk to my husband about it, but I really don't think he understood how I felt and thought I would just get over it like everyone else did. He was sensitive to the fact I had been dealt some hard knocks, but he really didn't know how it felt because it had never happened to him.

When I finally left for good, I was more prepared for the lack of support. I tried hard to stay strong, but it was bloody hard. Although my sister helped me with money for an apartment, I know she struggled with my decision to leave my husband and son, and she wasn't alone in those thoughts. I felt judged by others because I'd left my son with his father, but I didn't want to drag him around with me when I wasn't in a good space. I wanted him to have stability and have him keep his routine with his friends and school.

Not long after moving into the house near my son's school I had my fiftieth birthday. It's a big milestone in life and one that I hoped would be the next stage in my life. Little did I know that I was about to have more rocks thrown my way and some wounded me for a long time and pushed me further into the black hole.

A girlfriend of mine who lived overseas came back to Australia and said she would visit for my fiftieth birthday and stay at my house for a week or so. I was looking forward to having a good time with her, but, on her arrival, I soon found out her plan was to stay with me permanently. Because I was living on my own and had a spare room, she 'assumed' I would like her to stay.

This couldn't have been further from the truth.

I had made the mistake of telling her about the settlement money I'd received from my separation. It wasn't a huge amount of money but enough to make me feel I could probably buy a small unit to live in, and it was certainly not millions.

I picked her up from the airport and brought her home. Within a day of being at my house, she told me she had no money at all and asked if she could borrow some of mine. Big red flags went up and I felt sick at the thought of lending her money. She had been away for over twenty years, but we'd kept in touch and I considered her a friend. She knew all about the breakdown of my marriage and that I had moved out, and that's why she decided to visit me on her return to Australia. Or should I say, live with me!

I wasn't prepared for any of this. I was a mess and struggling with my own life, and if things were different and my life had been fine, I would have helped out, but I was dealing with so much that I simply didn't have the energy to help someone else. I had spent many years looking after my son and husband and had buried my own feelings and wellbeing. The reason I left my family was to find myself and heal and not be in a position where I was helping others.

Here I was looking forward to having a bit of fun with an old friend, but she thought she could stay with me permanently, and on top of that she had no money. She wanted me to help her out. If I'd known this before she arrived, I would have been straight with her then and not when everything went pear-shaped. The fact was, she lied to me about her return to Australia just being a holiday. Before her arrival I'd purchased extra food and a slab of beer as she wasn't a wine drinker, and within a day she had drunk the whole slab. While I know I was drinking too much, I could never drink that much beer in a day. I was scared at the thought of what she would be like if she had nothing to drink, but I wasn't going to fund her drinking habit.

When she asked for money, I told her I didn't have enough to lend her. She queried me about my settlement money from the sale of the family home, and I said it was all tied up in an account for a year so I couldn't access it. Yes, it was a lie, but I wasn't going to fund her lifestyle and have her keep asking me for more money. Because she lied about her return to Australia being a holiday when it wasn't, I felt I couldn't trust her to give me the money back. She then went and asked her aunt for money and applied for unemployment benefits.

So much for having a fun time when I turned fifty. It turned into a bloody nightmare that I simply couldn't deal with. When speaking to my sister about what had happened, she was furious that this so-called friend expected me to put her up at a time when I was going through my own life crisis. My sister knew I was looking forward to having a bit of fun for my fiftieth but realised that I wasn't going to be able to paint the town red with my friend as she had no money. She then organised a dinner with herself and a couple of my cousins. My friend didn't come along as it would have been embarrassing for her because my sister and cousins shouted me the dinner. I felt bad that she didn't come, and it put a dampener on the dinner. I was also stressed at the prospect of having someone live with me.

After a week I was beside myself and had to think of a way to get her out of my house. I didn't want her there. I knew the money she'd got from her aunt wasn't much and it would take weeks to get her benefits organised. I ended up telling her that my son wasn't comfortable with her living at my house and that it was important for me to be able to have my son stay with me. It wasn't a full-on lie as my son was not all that comfortable with her living there on a permanent basis. He was also of the understanding that she was only staying for a week or so. My son had been through enough and I was concerned about how he was coping with his parents' separation.

During our discussions I managed to find out more about what her plans were, and they were clearly about living with me, or should I say, living off me. She made out like I was the lost soul and that she wanted to help me but, unfortunately, she had her own agenda. Yes, I was a lost soul at the time, but I wasn't about to get help from someone who had a much bigger drinking problem than me and clearly had no money. She had no plans on what she was going to do and it became glaringly obvious that she thought I was going to help her get back on her feet because, well, I had money.

When I told her my son didn't want to stay with me while she was there, we spoke about her staying with her sister. She contacted her sister, who didn't even know she had returned to Australia, and she agreed that she could stay with her for a few days. That afternoon I drove her there. I felt really bad about what I was doing as I should have been helping her, but the whole situation was so stressful, and it was just adding to my depression and anxiety. I was also becoming angry about the situation I'd been placed in and that she'd lied to me about just coming for a visit for a week. I felt used and ultimately betrayed by someone I thought was a friend. She didn't consider my situation at all; it was all about helping herself out.

When I dropped her at her sister's, it was obvious that she wasn't happy about it either. Once again, I felt really bad, but I had to do what was good for me. The sister and I had a bit of small talk while taking her bags inside and she said, 'I'm guessing you're dumping her here?' I was shocked because I wanted to say, 'Yes'. On hearing her sister saying this, my friend said that she wouldn't be staying long and had some plans on staying with someone else. We said our goodbyes and I left.

On returning to my house and feeling awful about what I'd done, I went to my computer and scrolled through Facebook. My friend had been using my computer and she hadn't logged off her Facebook page. I was able to see her conversations with people she'd been keeping in contact with.

That's when I discovered she'd been bagging me to her friends about how I hadn't lent her money and how I'd gone out with my sister and cousins for my fiftieth and that she wasn't invited. The fact was that she didn't go because she had no money. Bloody hell! I had picked her up from the airport, fed her and supplied her with alcohol, plus a nice cosy bed to stay in and I was being called the bad person.

I received a message from her a couple of days later saying, 'Don't you love me anymore?' I was still very hurt that she had bagged me on Facebook in private messages to her mates. I decided to call her and say my piece. I didn't tell her about the Facebook messages but was honest about the fact I couldn't help her pick up her life back in Australia when I was busy trying to pick up the pieces of my own life. If my circumstances were different, and I wasn't in a downward spiral with my own life, I would have helped her out more. I said I was sorry, and she seemed to understand.

The next few days I saw more horrible messages and lies about me on Facebook, which were hurtful. In all of her messages to other friends she mentioned nothing about what was going on in my life; it was all about her and that I had let her down! That is when I closed her Facebook account so I couldn't access it again. I knew she had tried to take advantage of me, and that hurt, but I didn't feel bad anymore about dumping her at her sister's place.

A couple of weeks later, I received a card from her with $70 in it. All it said was, 'If I won a million dollars, I would give some to you.' The money was obviously a gesture at paying for her stay, which frankly was way more than $70 (one slab of beer cost $50) and something I never asked for, but the comment written on the card felt like a slap in the face that I didn't give her any money. I never heard from her again, nor did I want to.

Another close long-term friend interfered in the split with my husband and I, creating a situation that made our separation ten times worse than it should have been. This friend had known both of us since we were teenagers and caused so much extra pain for both of us that ultimately impacted our son. His actions towards both of us was nothing short of cruel, and the ramifications of his actions lasted for many years.

I still don't know, to this day, why this person inflicted more pain on us at a time when we were both coming to terms with the end of our marriage.

This friendship was a much greater loss than my friend who had returned from overseas, but I also realised that this person was angry and lost in the world and wanted to blame others for their difficulties in life. This person wanted to cause a lot of pain to justify their own pain.

Losing two long-term friends hit me hard as I had helped both of them a lot over many years. I never expected them to help me out, but I had hoped they would be, at least, someone to talk to and listen to me for once. I had realised that they were takers and not givers. Any type of friend or partnership is about give and take, but when people in your life constantly want to take, you have to let them go at some stage, otherwise they'll suck the life from you.

I'm not perfect by any stretch of the imagination as I, like many others, have made mistakes. Mistakes can make us learn and then hopefully you won't make them again. Sometimes you may have to learn a lesson more than once though. Not to say that is easy at all, mistakes or rejection can take a long time to get over, but you really do have to look at the person or the things they have done for you to understand. Once you see a clearer picture, only then can you move forward.

I truly think that I'm a good person and I try to do the right thing. I expect that others will do the same but, unfortunately, they often don't. You trust people and sometimes they let you down. When someone lets you down you can forgive them, but when they do it time and time again you really do have to let them go.

I've felt bad letting people go, but once you move on and they aren't in your life anymore you have more peace in your world and then you know you've done the right thing.

I have been way too trusting and it has cost me dearly. If someone who's hurt you changes and makes amends, then you can have them back in your life again, but you can't make someone change, they have to see for themselves that they have to change. If they don't, they are the ones who lose friends. Losing a friend can be like death; they may be still alive, but you just don't see them anymore. You try to remember the good times and not reflect on the bad because that will do your head in.

One friend who checked up on me and called to see if I was okay was a person who had dealt with a lot in their life. Her eldest son had died suddenly, and this is a pain that I never want to endure. Her strength was amazing and because of that I admire her greatly. Through her own pain she showed she cared and, frankly, that is all I wanted. Not for someone to pick me up and mend everything, but just someone who cared about what I was going through and understood that I was in great pain myself.

My sister did call often, but I know she struggled greatly with my depression. She has a busy life and hoped I would just get my act together and move on. I know she was worried, and she was the one who took the brunt of my anger. When I finally went on a higher dose of anti-depressants, I think she thought I would be fine but, sadly, I had a long way to go.

The other person who called me a lot was my mother-in-law. I knew that she loved me like a daughter, and she desperately wanted me to return to her son, but she always wanted to know if

I was okay. Our relationship had been rocky at first but over the years she knew I was a giving person and had helped her family a lot. The fact was, I had more to do with my husband's family than my own. I sometimes think that people may have been easier on me if I'd left my husband for another man, then people would have understood why I'd left. Just leaving didn't make sense to anyone.

My mother-in-law hoped we would reconcile and, due to her being a religious person, I don't doubt she prayed for it to happen.

I respected her so much that she cared enough to call me. Unlike the rest of the family, as I never heard from any of them. That hurt more than you can imagine. A family I had been a part of for over thirty years didn't seem to give me a second thought. It was over two years before I saw them again and sadly that was at my mother-in-law's funeral. It was difficult to see them all again, but I wanted to go to the funeral out of respect to her.

The family were all nice and asked me how I was. Some of the extended family were happy to see me, but I felt like I never took a breath the whole time I was at the funeral and then the wake. My son was surprised I went as he was well aware that none of them had ever been in contact with me. He thought I was brave to go. I really don't think they resented me or disliked me for leaving my husband, I just don't think they understood why I'd left, like most other people. But it hurt like hell that I wasn't contacted, just to ask if I was okay. It was another thing that I had to grieve, and this time it was the loss of an entire family.

Being loved, liked and nurtured is something we all crave in life as we need to have a sense of belonging and being needed and wanted. I felt alone and unwanted and that I wasn't worthy of love. I think that most people thought I was tough and strong and able to deal with everything that came my way.

I have learnt that true friends are hard to find. They are out there but be wary of the ones who take and are not prepared to give.

One faithful, trusty friend and companion was my beautiful Sophie, a female Rhodesian ridgeback/Staffordshire cross, who saved my life. She was the family dog I took ownership of as my husband worked full-time and my son was a growing teenager who was busy with his own life, so Sophie was better off with me. She absolutely loved the beach, something she didn't go to often when I lived in Melbourne. She knew when I was sad and would sit on the couch with me and snuggle in. She was the one who got me off the couch each day to take her for a walk along the beach. I was devastated when she passed away. I would like to think that the last couple of years of her life she had a nice retirement by the beach, and she was a happy dog. She was fourteen when she passed away, a good innings for a dog her size.

At the time when I couldn't trust 'people' friends, she was the one who was constantly by my side. Dogs give such unconditional love, and I really don't understand how some people can treat pets so badly. Sophie was a rescue dog from the RSPCA and she had her own issues. Butter wouldn't melt in her mouth when she was with me, but she didn't like other dogs and was very protective of me.

Pets are the best thing to have if you have any type of health issues. It is well documented that pets are great companions and particularly when it comes to mental health. They give you such love and they rely on you to look after them and that gives you self-worth.

Giving to yourself is your first priority; if you don't look after yourself first you are unable to look after others. I feel that Sophie looked after me and helped me heal and for that I will be forever grateful to have had her in my life. She now lies in rest in a silver container with her collar around it and a beautiful picture of her, while on the beach, with a smile on her face.

My friend said to me once that when dogs pass away, they leave pawprints on your heart. I can assure you that Sophie certainly did that.

Like any illness you have to overcome, it takes time to heal, and depression and anxiety are no different. The one thing that is different is that when you have an illness that affects the body, like cancer or if you've had a car accident and are badly injured, people have more sympathy for you. They visit you in the hospital, give you flowers, drop food off at your house and ask if you need anything to just call.

Having a mental illness is different. When you have a mental illness, most people cannot see that something is wrong. If they see you are not yourself and a bit sad, they think you're just having a bit of a downer and you will get over it. From my experience, I've seen firsthand that many people will walk the other way as they just don't know how to deal with someone who is sad and not coping with life. Some friends I'd known for over thirty years turned their back on me and didn't even call to see if I was okay.

I do get that it can be difficult to deal with someone who has depression, but if you do know someone who isn't coping with life, just give them a call and see how they are; it can make a world of difference.

Chapter 17

The final straw

After a year and when my son had finished his final year at school, I had to decide where I was going to live. I wanted to purchase a small place in Melbourne, but when I looked, all I could afford was a small dog box in the outer suburbs. I knew living in a place like that wouldn't be good for me, but if I wanted to be near my son then that was what I would have to do.

As my good friend had a holiday house in a beautiful coastal town only an hour and a half from Melbourne, I stayed there a few times and fell in love with the place. It was so peaceful, and I loved being near the ocean, something I wouldn't be able to do in Melbourne. My son was at an age where he was partying hard with his friends, and I knew that wherever I purchased, he wouldn't be living with me. His father had purchased a house in a suburb not that far from the family home we'd sold. I knew he would want to be close to the city and his friends and therefore it would be better for him to stay with his father.

I looked at some houses in the seaside town and found I could actually get a small house for a great price. I really didn't want to stay in Melbourne as the life I was living there was shitsville. I really wanted to change my life.

When I spoke to my son about moving out of Melbourne, he told me that all he wanted was for me to be happy, and if moving away from Melbourne was going to do that, he was all for it. I know that he didn't want to be moving from house to house and this way he could come and stay with me if he wanted to get away from the big smoke and have a break down on the beach.

Once I knew my son was okay with me moving away from Melbourne, I set about looking for a place before my lease was up on the house I was renting. The last thing I wanted was to have to move back to my parents' place and then move again into my new house. I had moved four times in two years, and I needed stability more than ever.

I managed to find a modest house that needed some work but it had good bones. It was classified as a three-bedroom home, but the third bedroom was really small and not what I would consider a bedroom. It had two bathrooms; a small ensuite off the main bedroom and your regular-sized bathroom that's in most small houses, a small kitchen and lounge area plus a little garden that needed a lot of work as it had been neglected. As I'd renovated my family home I was, what I would call, a 'tradie chick' and more than happy to get my hands dirty.

I managed to purchase the house a lot cheaper than it was advertised for and subsequently got myself a great deal. The bonus was that I still had money in the bank to fix the place up. Everything fell into place, and I moved straight from the rental house into my new beachside haven in 2014.

Most people thought I was mad (I probably was at the time), but I saw it as a new start. Somewhere I could 'find myself' (yes, that cheesy saying again) and begin to heal.

Moving away doesn't take the pain away; it moves with you, and as much as I felt happy in my new place, I still had more obstacles in my path to overcome.

They say that sometimes you have to hit rock bottom before you can start to come back up, and when I moved, as much as I thought I had already hit rock bottom, I still had a little bit more to go before I was face down in the bottom of the pit.

I had started to look for work and, luckily, within a couple of months I found a part-time casual job at a local resort. I really hadn't expected to find work that quickly, but I needed the money and being on unemployment benefits wasn't something I wanted to continue.

After working at the resort for about eighteen months, I started to look for jobs on a more permanent basis. The money at the resort was crappy and you didn't know if you were going to get work due to the position being on a casual basis. But I was glad I only worked part-time as I wasn't ready for full-time work as I was still dealing with my depression and I had the occasional anxiety attack at work. I used to hide in the toilet and try to get it together. One of the other ladies I worked with picked up on it a couple of times and always asked if I was okay. She was a sweet person, a giver. There didn't seem to be many other temporary jobs around, unlike working in the city where they were plentiful. I hated the process of looking for a permanent job as I had done it so many times, but at least I had it down pat.

For the last couple of years I had continued to see my psychologist, and she was wonderful. The fact is, you do most of the talking and they give some direction, but it's ultimately up to you to do the work. I think for the first year all I did was cry through each session as I didn't really cry in front of anyone else. My true feelings flowed out when I was with her. I cried about how pathetic I was for losing so many jobs, the end of my marriage, leaving my son behind, the hurt from friends and family that they didn't understand what I was going through.

I cried *a lot*.

I used to go home straight away after a session and hide away because if anyone saw me, they would know something was wrong as I looked like shit. My eyes used to be so puffed up they felt like they were going to pop out of my head. I kept seeing the psychologist until I moved into my seaside house. When I told her I was moving out of Melbourne I don't know if she really thought it was a good idea. Frankly, I think I was running away and wanted to be as far away as possible from my life in Melbourne.

I knew I still needed help and started seeing another psychologist in the area. I found that seeing someone 'local' wasn't a good idea as she would talk about things happening in the local area and some of our discussions were just drivel. She wasn't helping and frankly I think she just liked to have a chat. I found getting good help in regional areas hard, not just when it came to mental health issues but with anything you needed when it came to being sick.

The GP I was seeing in the area was wonderful though (a rare find). She helped me with another mental health plan so I could get more subsidised sessions from a psychologist, and she also convinced me to increase my anti-depressants. I knew that I had to, as my depression wasn't getting any better and it was hard finding my way in the area.

I had met some new people in town and also got involved with the local theatre group, helping out with sets. It was great to be involved in community events. Despite this, I didn't really do much else and stayed at home a lot. I was doing a lot of work on my house trying to fix it up and put my stamp on it, but other than that I really didn't go out much at all. I felt lonely sometimes but on the other hand spending time alone was peaceful for me, and I needed that at the time. The past couple of years had been awful dealing with lots of rejection from people I thought cared. I saw people differently now, and I had lost a lot of trust in the human race.

Finally, I applied for a customer service position at a large food manufacturer in the area. I had looked up this company and saw that it was a growing business, and it had a manufacturing facility in the area. The website had a lot of comments on how the company operated and how it valued the staff and encouraged training to further enhance careers within the organisation. I had seen this rhetoric before, but I thought working for a business in the country things might be different.

I updated my CV and typed up a covering letter and emailed it to them. About a week later I got a call from the HR manager and I was asked if I'd do a psychological test (which was becoming the norm when it came to the job interview process). It was sent to me by an employment agency, and I had to answer questions online and submit it for assessment. I did think, *Well, this will be interesting; I wonder if I'll appear as a nut case*. I had been through so much in the past few years: leaving my husband, moving to the country, leaving my son behind and all the jobs that I'd had over the years, which had all made me insecure about myself. I was still adjusting to living in a country town and meeting new people.

When the results came back from the psychological test, I had high scores for reliability, confidence and also being extremely experienced in customer relations. I was surprised by the confidence side as I felt that I'd lost so much over the years and my self-worth was very low.

The HR manager called and an interview was arranged with the newly appointed marketing manager. I had two separate interviews – one with the new marketing manager and then later one with the HR officer and the transport manager. About two weeks later, I received the phone call that I'd got the job. I was over the moon as I would finally be earning some decent money.

I felt like everything was finally going my way for a change and I was looking forward to starting a new job and earning a decent wage. Living on benefits and doing part-time work was hard financially. Lucky I didn't go out much as I really didn't have the money to spend.

I was excited about starting my new job as this position was suited to my skills and experience. It was a newly created position within the business, but I knew I was more than qualified to do the job. I would be looking after clients' orders and coordinating their deliveries. I did think it was strange that they didn't have someone doing this already as any company that has clients usually has a customer service department, but for some strange reason, they didn't.

On the first day at my new job, I was greeted by the marketing manager, who had been working for the company for about two months. The office was cramped and a desk had been set up in the corner for me next to the window. The usual things were on the desk: computer, in-tray, pens and so on. I was introduced to the two women sitting near me, and one of them was going to train me on the ordering system. She had only been there for about four months and was employed on a temporary basis to place orders into the system.

For the first couple of hours, it was about setting up my computer with passwords and access. I had a bit of a play around on the computer for a little while, just navigating the system and getting an understanding of the program they had. After lunch the woman who was training me gave me a manual and said, 'Here you go, just read this and follow the instructions.' I thought, *Okay*, so I read through them and tried to follow the instructions. The manual was antiquated and the ordering system seemed complicated. I had worked in so many places and always found it easy to pick up the ordering system, but this was an old and complicated program and clearly needed to be upgraded.

I decided to talk to someone in the IT division as I wasn't getting a lot of help from my trainer. There were three people working in one room and when we discussed the ordering system, they were very frank in saying it was, well, fucked. They went on to say that the whole computer network in the building kept crashing because of the way orders were being placed. The transport division used a program that couldn't handle the amount of information being placed in it and that is why the system kept crashing. They had told management that the program should be removed and replaced but management had done nothing about it. They were hoping I would have some impact in making these changes happen, and that I would convince management that the current system was impacting customers' orders being delivered. This is when I realised why my position had been created as there was simply no one coordinating orders between the factory and the transport division. They helped me understand what was going on, and I could see that they were correct in stating that the system was fucked.

I went back to my desk and asked my trainer if she had time to go through a few things. She said she would when all the orders were in. I then asked her if I could watch her placing the orders on the system, and she reluctantly agreed. She was going through everything so fast and not explaining anything, and I started to wonder if she wanted to train me at all. Later that day I found out this woman was going on holidays for three weeks and no one else had time to train me. I thought, *Great!* I had just started a new job and the person who was meant to train me was going on holidays!

This job was not off to a good start. I did as much as I could in the first week, but I was given little time with my so-called trainer as she was just too busy making sure everything was up to date before she went away. Frankly, I thought it was ridiculous that a person who was only a temporary fill-in was allocated to train me at all.

At the end of my first week, I was leaving to go home, heading for my car when I noticed that this woman was sitting in her car. As I walked past her, I waved and said, 'Hope you have a nice break.' She opened her window and said, 'Yes I will, and good luck, you're going to need it.' I smiled at her as I walked away but the sick feeling in the pit of my stomach told me that working for this company was going to be very difficult.

I knew that the first couple of months were going to be challenging, not unlike most jobs when learning a new position, but this was on a whole new level than I had experienced before.

The following Monday I spoke to the marketing manager and told him that the person meant to train me was now on holiday. He told me he'd had no idea she was going on holidays and that I should have started when she was back. *Well, no shit*, I thought, *but what am I supposed to do now?* The fact that nobody had told my manager this person was going on holiday highlights the lack of communication that was going on in the company.

I continued to read through the manual I'd been given and tried to put some orders through. Due to the company exporting some of their products overseas, the orders were not clear when it came to the prices. When I tried to ask questions, nobody had time to spend with me. The other lady who sat near me was so busy she got angry when I asked a question, so I stopped asking her. The other people in the office couldn't help as they didn't know how to place orders either.

The two salespeople were like polar opposites; one was friendly but the other was rude and abrupt when he spoke to me. After a couple of days, he asked me if I'd put all of his orders in. I said they weren't finished as I was still learning and nobody was helping me. I didn't want to put orders into the system incorrectly as they were mostly for export, and if they were wrong it would be a nightmare to fix as it took up to eight weeks for them to be shipped. If they were wrong, it would cost the company a lot of money.

Well, he went straight to the marketing manager and complained that I wasn't doing my job. I had only been there a week!

After having a discussion with my manager, he agreed that the situation wasn't good, but he did nothing to fix it. He just told me to sit it out for three weeks until the other lady came back.

Great strategy, I thought. Sit it out when I was being bullied by the salesperson, who wanted everything done yesterday, and when it wasn't done, he would complain about me. Yes, that's a great way to deal with it, not!

One of the men in the manufacturing area knew I was struggling and that no one was helping me, so he organised a tour around the factory so that I'd have a better understanding of the company's operations. I was appreciative that he gave me some time to show me around (something that should have happened in the first week) and that at least someone could see I needed assistance. He was helpful and friendly. He spent most of the day showing me around as there was a lot to see and comprehend.

While walking around, he did warn me about one person, who didn't like the fact that my position had been created and that I should be careful of her. The unfortunate thing was that this person was a control freak, and I found out quickly that she was unliked by everyone. Within two weeks of being there I had four people warn me about her, and that I needed to watch my back. Things were just getting worse by the day, and I thought that I should just leave, but I needed the money and hoped things would improve.

The salesperson who was demanding was, frankly, a bully. Not just to me but to others in the company, and naturally he was also disliked because he wanted everything done yesterday. He did everything last minute and expected everyone else to push things through, which only created mistakes. So many of his orders were made incorrectly in the time he had worked for the company, and many of them sat in storage and couldn't be sold or had to be re-worked. I later found out there was a whole warehouse full of his crap and nobody talked about it.

I set up a meeting with the production manager to find out what was happening to some customers' orders, and it was obvious he wasn't happy that I was asking questions about production issues. I stayed calm as I said, 'I'm not doing this to have a go at you. I've been asked to get answers to these, and I also need to understand why it happened.' He seemed to calm down a bit and understand that I was just trying to do my job. He answered a few questions and said he would get back to me on the others, which he never did.

On a weekly basis we had a production meeting with staff members from various departments to go over late orders, production issues and delays. I had to run this meeting and note all the answers from the various departments. I was nervous at the first meeting as I had only been in the job for a couple of weeks and still didn't really have a good understanding of the company, which is only natural. The fact that they wanted me to run this meeting was ridiculous as I didn't know what was going on as nobody was prepared to tell me anything.

The vibe in the meeting was extremely unpleasant and I didn't get answers to any of the problems going on with orders; the meeting was a joke. Some of these complaints were up to six months old, and it was obvious things were just going around in circles. Due to the fact I was being pressured into getting the complaints sorted out, I was sending out emails to try to get some answers. Well, that was a mistake. I was subsequently inundated with emails, which mostly repeated themselves, as I'd been cc'd on every email that was sent from the various departments. Everyone was just trying to cover their arses; it was so obvious.

After three weeks, a couple of men were contracted to sort out the systems within the organisation, as they were about to be taken over by another company. Due to a recent audit, it must have become obvious to the company taking over the business that a lot of things needed to change before they finalised the sale. The consultants organised so many meetings it was out of control, and because I was the main customer service person (the only one actually) I was asked to go to most of the meetings. Here I was, only three weeks in, no training, and I wasn't able to spend time on putting orders into the system. I don't think the consultants were aware of the fact that I had only just started with the company, and they assumed I knew more about how the business operated.

The marketing manager was doing nothing to help me get assistance with the job, so I spoke to the general manager about the fact I couldn't keep up with orders and that going to all of these meetings was hindering me greatly in doing my job. He was aware that I wasn't getting any training, and that the transport manager wasn't happy I'd been employed with the company. We also discussed the issue that I was being bullied by one of the salespeople and he was constantly complaining to my manager that I wasn't doing my job. I thought I had someone who would do something to help me but, unfortunately, all he gave me was lip service. He did absolutely nothing.

Over the next few weeks, I worked overtime plus came in on Saturdays when I didn't have to go to any bloody meetings, and I would catch up on orders. All of my orders had to be checked by the transport manager, but she took her time, of course, and her handwritten notes were so small I needed a magnifying glass to read them. Having seen her handwriting on other things in the office, it was obvious she was making my job even more difficult. It was becoming clear to me that she didn't want me working for the company.

After five weeks in the job, the woman who was meant to train me had returned from holidays. I was hoping I could get more help from her, but I was dreaming. Due to her reporting to the transport manager, she was told that she wasn't able to help me as she had been assigned a new job to do.

So, there it was, I was left to drown on my own.

I made the decision to see the occupational health and safety officer and see if she could help. I didn't want to go to the woman in HR as she was good friends with the transport manager, and besides that she wouldn't even talk to me in the lunchroom. I had no idea why she didn't want to talk to me but then I noticed that she didn't speak to anyone while in the lunchroom. It had nothing to do with me at all, she just never chatted to anyone and all she did was play on her phone. Here was a person who was meant to help and assist people with their jobs, but she was as cold as ice. She was a perfect example of someone who shouldn't be in HR.

When I saw the OHS officer, she didn't seem surprised at what was happening to me. She told me the company was difficult to work for and she'd also had many difficulties when she started as most of the men didn't seem to like the fact they had to listen to a woman about safety issues. That was when I broke into tears. All the pressure and stress had built up and I just let it all out. She was so nice and sympathetic and said she would go and speak with the newly appointed HR manager, who was currently in training (interesting that he got training and not me) and see what could be arranged with regard to me getting the training I required to perform my job.

I had no idea a new HR manager had even been employed. After a couple of days, I had a meeting with the HR manager and we went over a list of things I required. We then had a meeting with my manager and from there I was allocated time with various people to undergo the training I should have had in the first place.

Over the next few weeks, I met with some of these people, but a lot had to cancel due to their work commitments. I continued to do overtime (unpaid, of course) and after about six weeks I was finally starting to get a handle on things. Not bad as far as I was concerned, considering I'd had little to no training. The orders were up to date and a new system was being tested by the IT department so it wouldn't keep crashing. They actually thanked me for raising the issue with the general manager and that finally the pathetic programs they had were being addressed.

I did notice that my boss was starting to act differently towards me, but I just put it down to the fact that everyone was under pressure and all departments were being questioned by consultants on how and why things were done the way they were. It was clear that most of the companies' procedures were not working, and a lot needed to change to make it run smoothly.

The consultants were finally making some headway into setting processes to make the factory run more efficiently. It was decided at one meeting that the sales department needed to be in the loop regarding production issues, so we could keep customers informed of any delays. This happened in most companies I'd worked for, but this company had no such process – it was no wonder my position was created.

So, after six weeks in a job that was newly created, I was the person who had to keep things in line and ask questions if orders were not on time so I could advise customers. I couldn't believe it. The consultants obviously thought I was up to it, even though I hadn't worked with the company for long. I did ask a lot of questions at the meetings, unlike most people who just kept quiet. During these meetings you could see a lot of the other staff members weren't happy about me being kept in the loop about production issues and that the consultants were referring to me as the 'gatekeeper'.

By the end of my seventh week, I had a meeting set up with the new HR manager and my boss to go over how my training was going. As far as I was concerned, I was learning this job on my own but felt I had done well under the circumstances. I was hoping that after a meeting with the consultants I might actually get the training I needed. The consultants wanted me to have more control over orders so that I could keep customers informed of any delays, and they were keen to get new procedures in place.

As I walked to the HR manager's office with my folder to take some notes, I felt this sick feeling in the pit of my stomach. As I approached the door, the HR manager came out and told me to wait a second as he just needed to photocopy something. When I finally walked into the office, the marketing manager was sitting at the table. The discussion was short, very short, and then my manager said, 'Linda, I've made the decision to let you go as you don't "fit in".' That's all he said, then he just sat there looking at me.

I sat there totally stunned. The HR manager said nothing, and both men just looked at me. I was silent for about a minute (but it felt like forever). I kept my composure and finally said, 'Do you mind if I have a minute to myself.' I wanted to say more but the words would not come out of my mouth; I was in complete shock.

The HR manager said, 'Of course,' and they both stood up and left the room. I just sat there for about five minutes and then got up and walked out of the office. The HR manager was waiting for me, but the marketing manager had run for his fucking life. He knew I had more to say and because he also knew that I hadn't been trained, something he admitted to me on a number of occasions. So, he did a runner to avoid any type of confrontation with me. He was the person who created this position and employed me, and he did nothing to help me and left me to drown. He was well aware of all the difficulties I was having getting training and also all the problems that the company was having with the takeover of the business.

The only reason for my dismissal was because I didn't 'fit in'. What did he mean by 'fit in'? Pathetic excuse really considering how hard I'd worked trying to do the job without any assistance. I guess that is the only thing he could think of saying at the time. I do believe that because he was also new to the company, and he created a new position as a customer service coordinator (which was badly needed), he had been given a hard time by others within the company. Everyone there was concerned about the takeover of the company, and they were all a bit worried about their own positions. The decision by the consultants to make me the 'gatekeeper' when I was so new to the company didn't help.

When the marketing manager walked out of the office, I never saw him again. I am convinced he hid somewhere in the office so I couldn't find him. He had no regard for my welfare at all, he didn't give a shit and neither did the HR manager. It was a cruel dismissal, and the new HR manager obviously wasn't suited to the job as he didn't even ask me if I was okay or if there was anything I needed to know. All he said was, 'I need to follow you upstairs so you can collect your personal belongings. I'll stand back so it's not obvious what's happening.'

Gee, thanks!

The HR manager had only started working for the company about two weeks after I started, and he had absolutely no idea what was really going on. He was not at any of the meetings I attended as he wasn't part of the sales and production areas. He was just doing his job as a witness to my dismissal and that was it.

I went upstairs and into the kitchen to get my lunch out of the fridge. I must have looked like a zombie as one of the men from the maintenance area asked if I was okay, and then I just burst into tears. He asked me what was wrong, and I told him I'd just been sacked. He just stood there looking at me in shock and said, 'Why?' I told him that apparently I didn't 'fit in'. He clearly didn't know what to say but he followed me out of the kitchen and gave me a hug and wished me good luck. As I let go of him and turned around, I saw the HR manager standing there watching me like a hawk. I said goodbye to the maintenance man and then walked to my desk.

Nobody in the office took much notice of me as I picked up my bag and got a couple of personal items out of the drawer. One of the consultants was sitting at the desk next to me, and we'd often spoken, just general stuff like what we'd done on the weekend, saying good morning/night and just general interaction. I have no doubt he noticed that not a lot of interaction went on in the office as most people kept to themselves. He could probably feel the toxic vibe as well. As I was about to walk out, I tapped him on the shoulder and asked if he had a minute. He stood up and we walked into the hallway.

The HR manager was hovering around and looked a bit shocked to see me with the consultant but said nothing and just watched me walk into the hallway. I told the consultant what had just happened, and that I'd just been dismissed. He was clearly stunned and didn't know what to say. It had only been finalised a couple of days before that I would be the 'gatekeeper', and now I'd been dismissed. He hugged me and wished me all the best as he could see the HR manager hovering and didn't want to make a scene.

As I walked down the stairs, the lady from accounts saw I was upset and asked if I was okay. I just told her I'd been sacked and kept walking down the stairs. She walked down the stairs with me and said, 'This is one fucked-up place.' On my way out I decided to say goodbye to the OHS lady as she was the only one who was really sympathetic to my situation. She was stunned at what had happened. She could see the HR manager was in the distance but asked me why. I told her it was because I didn't 'fit in'. She just shook her head and didn't know what to say. She hugged me and just said, 'Arseholes'. The HR manager wasn't close enough to hear it.

So, in about fifteen minutes, I'd had four people hug me and look totally shocked that I'd been dismissed. The newly appointed HR manager would have been looking on and seeing that people actually liked me. I wonder what must have been going through his head. I hope he was also thinking that this situation was really fucked up.

The lady from accounts walked with me to the security area. I handed in my pass to the man on the desk. I was a mess and had tears pouring down my face as I handed it in. The security guy also asked what'd happened and said it in a manner like he thought something had happened to a family member, like a death or something. When handing over my security pass I just said, 'They just sacked me.' He was a lovely man and always cheerful, but he'd warned me about the transport manager, along with other people. I told him what had happened, and he stood there stunned, just like all the others.

I felt that the transport manager had a lot to do with it; she had her nose out of joint from the start and hated the fact this new position was created. It took away the control she had when it came to how orders were being processed. In all my time working for so many organisations I had never worked for a company where the transport manager had so much control over customers' orders. This company desperately needed a customer service coordinator, but it clearly upset her that this process was being taken away from her. Also, the fact I was going to be made the gatekeeper when it came to having control over orders. She clearly was in a spin and, as far as I'm concerned, she did everything in her power to make sure I was dismissed.

The day the consultants put procedures in place that I would be the so-called gatekeeper, they may as well have put a target on my back. I was a goner. The consultants had no idea about the dynamics of the company. They obviously thought I was more than capable of doing the job, which I was, but they had no idea what was going on behind the scenes.

I said goodbye to the security man, and the accounts lady walked me outside the gate. By this time, I was sobbing and could barely speak. She asked me if I was going to be okay to drive home. I said, 'Probably not,' and then thanked her and walked to my car. I sat in the car for a couple of minutes just trying to get my composure back, then I drove off. The drive home was on a windy road and down the hills to the coastline where I lived. While driving down the hill I did think that I should just drive off the side of the road and then the pain would stop.

I had just been pushed further into the black hole.

Chapter 18

Beyond blue

When I finally got home I opened a bottle of wine and just curled up on the couch and sobbed. I didn't ring anyone. Once again, I was embarrassed, humiliated and rejected, and the fact I had lost another job made the shame rise up and hit me like an axe. Every time I had lost a job, the discrimination, the sexual harassment, the bullying, plus the lack of support during my marriage breakup, it was all too hard. It was me – it must be me – why this kept happening. I felt that I couldn't do this anymore, and nobody cared anyway. If I took my own life, I would be doing everyone a favour as they wouldn't have to deal with me.

Over the years I often contemplated taking my own life. I was so unhappy, but the only thing that kept me going was my son. Whenever I thought of how I was going to take my own life, I thought of him. But this time it was so much harder. He was older now and wasn't a little boy anymore. He lived with his father in the city, and he was out living his life, as he should. As much as our relationship was good, I felt that he was slipping away from me as most children do when they get older.

After a couple of weeks of hating myself and thinking something was wrong with me, I drove to the hardware store and purchased a long tube that was mainly used for attaching to a washing machine. But I wasn't going to use it for the washing machine. I had made my plan on how I was going to take my life.

I got home and took the heavy-duty tape from my kitchen drawer. I moved the car into the driveway behind my high wooden gate so that nobody could see what I was doing. I then got a towel and also picked up my dogs' blanket that she slept on and placed it in the car. I taped up the tube to the exhaust pipe of the car and then placed it through the window. I stuffed the gap of the window with the towel as I had to make sure it was blocked. I then put my beautiful dog, who I thought was my only friend, into the car, and then I sat down in the driver's seat. I kissed my dog and turned on the engine. I could not deal with the pain anymore; I could not go through this again. What was wrong with me? Why did this happen to me all the time? *It's me,* I thought, *I know it's me. It's all my fault.*

I had left no note, nothing. I thought that nobody cared anyway, and it would be weeks before anyone found me. Nobody visited me so that was also why I was taking the dog with me, as I couldn't let her starve to death. We would both go together.

Then thoughts of my son came to mind. I loved him so much. How would he deal with this? His relationship with his father wasn't great at the time. Who would he talk to? I also thought of a close work colleague who I spoke with a couple of weeks before he took his own life. In this discussion he told me he'd tried to take his life. I remember telling him his kids needed him. He did tell me that when he had tried to take his life, he saw a picture of his kids and couldn't go through with it. Unfortunately, he did go through with it. I remember seeing his children at his funeral and feeling so sad for them that they had lost their father and the fact that they had to live with thoughts of how their father died and having people ask, 'How did your dad die?'

That is when I turned the ignition off. I continued to sit in the car for a while sobbing uncontrollably. I got out of the car, let my dog out then went back inside the house. That is when I made the decision to ring Beyond Blue. This was difficult for me to do as I had to finally admit to myself that I was in a really bad way. I knew I couldn't ring anyone in my family as they'd think I was just being overly dramatic. They used to call me a drama queen when I was young.

Beyond Blue is an organisation that helps people with depression and those who're considering self-harm. When I called the number, I got a lady on the line, and she sounded about my age. We spoke about what had happened and that I'd lost my job, and how I'd set up the car to take my life. She knew I needed help and asked me if there was anyone nearby that could come over. I said no. I had told nobody I'd lost my job. From there, she obviously knew I needed to get to the hospital where I could be watched. She asked if I needed an ambulance, and I told her I'd make my way to the local hospital, which was only fifteen minutes away, and I most certainly wasn't going to have an ambulance in front of my house. She told me that she would contact the hospital to ensure they knew I was coming.

When I got there, they had been informed of my arrival. I was put into a private room and just lay on the bed sobbing. I think I had continually cried for about two weeks by this point, so I must have looked like shit. Not long later, a psychologist came to see me. All I could say was, 'I don't want to be here anymore.' We spoke about my job losses and the end of my marriage, and she asked me if I wanted her to contact anyone. She wanted me to go to a psychiatric hospital to be assessed and also to be in a safe area where I wasn't alone to attempt suicide. I really didn't want to call anyone; I just wanted the pain to go away and not involve anybody in what I was going through. I didn't think they cared anyway, but I eventually gave her my sister's number.

Within about an hour and a half, my sister was at the hospital. She was totally blown away by how I looked, and she was also a bit shocked I had lost my job and hadn't told her. We had a good relationship but there was a lot I hadn't told her over the years. Well, a lot I hadn't told anyone. She did listen to me on the phone, but like a lot of people, she was busy with her life. She knew I needed more help but didn't know what to do. She didn't understand how much pain I was in. When you're so low and finding it hard to get out of bed, all you want to do is drink to forget the pain. Nobody really listened to me, but I also found it difficult to tell others everything that had gone on in my life. I considered myself a bit of a loser because everything seemed to go wrong.

Most of the time I listened to everyone else's problems, and, to be honest, nobody ever really asked how I was. I suppose in some ways I thought my life was not as bad as some people's. My friend who had to deal with the tragedy of losing her son had to deal with such pain and grief; I never thought my pain could be worse than hers. But as she said to me one day, 'Everyone has some pain in their lives, we all have to deal with it at some time in our life.' Just because what had occurred to her was extremely painful didn't mean my pain was any less. She is such a treasured friend; I am lucky to have her in my life.

I have suffered great loss over the years. Not just jobs (albeit many) but the loss of my marriage and nobody understanding why I left my husband. I left my son behind with my husband only because I knew I was spinning out of control and needed to get my act together. The loss of so-called friends who couldn't give a shit about me. I had two close friends treat me so badly that it made me fall into the deep dark hole even further. I grieved the loss of my husband's family. My family didn't know how bad I was when I left my husband. They thought I would be okay, I guess. I had moved to another part of the state, mainly to run away, but now I think it was because I knew I was going to have to do this on my own.

Ultimately, you have to fix yourself. You can hope that you will have some support along the way from either family or friends, but you are the one that has to dig yourself out of the hole. Some people get a lot of help when faced with such darkness, but some don't manage to dig themselves out of it and, subsequently, they take their own lives.

I had dealt with so much rejection that I felt I wasn't worthy of anything good happening to me. In some ways I thought maybe I was a bad person, and I deserved all this shit that was happening to me.

Later that night the psych counsellor managed to get me into a psych ward. My sister agreed to take me there. It was very late by this stage, but I was told that if I didn't go that night, the bed wouldn't be available tomorrow. So, we drove about an hour to get there. It was late when we arrived. I was taken to my room and then it hit me.

I was in a psychiatric hospital; this is where my life had led me.

A FUCKING PSYCH WARD.

Chapter 19

The doctor merry-go-round

It was the middle of the night before we arrived at the psychiatric hospital, and I was starting to panic at the thought of where I was going. I could have changed my mind, but I didn't want to be a burden on anyone.

Before going to the hospital, we had dropped into my house to pick up a few clothes and toiletries. I gave my dog some food and water and my sister picked her up the next day and had her looked after by my parents as she was familiar with their house.

Due to it being so late when we arrived, we had to press the intercom buzzer and speak to a nurse, who had been informed about my arrival. The nurse had to go through everything and make sure I didn't have any items that they didn't allow. My shoelaces were removed from my shoes and most of my jewellery was taken, and they searched for any sharp objects. Oh, and of course they took my mobile phone. Before my sister left, we spoke about informing my son about where I was. I couldn't call him and at that stage I had no idea of how to contact him, seeing as my phone had been taken from me. I really wasn't thinking about much at all as I was in a daze. I was so tired and making decisions about anything just simply didn't enter my head.

As I entered the hallway, the lights were dim as all the other patients were in bed. It was quiet but also felt eerie and sparse. Iwas taken to my room and that is when I really started to panic about where I was. I started to cry again. The nurse gave me

Valium to calm me down and help me sleep. She told me I was in the women's section and that no men were allowed in and that I would be safe. I could hear someone screaming and making a commotion down the hall, and I asked the nurse what was going on. She told me the facility took in a lot of drug addicts because they didn't have anywhere else to go. She went on to say that because emergency departments couldn't keep them, they got sent to the psychiatric wards. She told me I was lucky to get a bed as most people couldn't access them because there simply weren't enough available.

As I looked around towards the nurses' station, I could see two large and muscular men, who would clearly take over if a patient got out of control. Most of the other nurses were women.

The nurse left after I'd settled down a bit and my Valium was kicking in. You couldn't lock your door, and even when you did shut it, a large gap at the bottom let light in. The room had a single bed, a chair and a small cupboard to put my things into. The shower and toilet were down the hall and you shared with the other women. Everything was made so you couldn't harm yourself and that made it even more obvious where you were. It was not like a normal hospital room: it was sparse and didn't even have a picture on the wall, and definitely no TV. Even in the bathroom there were no mirrors, only steel plates so at least you could see yourself – like the ones in a lot of public toilets – because of course no glass was allowed, and we even drank out of plastic cups.

The next morning, I had a different nurse come and check on me and she showed me around. There was a lounge area for women only, with a big window that looked onto the nurses' station. It had a television, books and lots of puzzles. Then we went into the common area through a sensor door that required a card swipe to get back in. I was given the card so I could come and go from the dining room and small outdoor area. We then went into the kitchen area, where you could make a coffee or tea. The water was lukewarm, and no cutlery was available, only wooden icy-pole sticks so you could stir your coffee; another reminder that you couldn't harm yourself.

There was a small outdoor area with rubber flooring and some seats so you could at least sit in the sun and get some fresh air as you couldn't leave the building without supervision. We then went to the dining area where breakfast was being served. The nurse left me so that she could attend to something else. That is when I saw most of the other patients. Some looked up and watched me get some toast and a cup of tea. I never spoke, and I tried not to have eye contact with anyone while I was looking around the room. After breakfast I returned to the women's lounge, picked up a puzzle and started to lay the pieces out on a small table. A couple of other women walked in and one of them introduced herself and asked me a few questions about where I was from and what I was 'in' for. It sounded like I was in prison, well, maybe it was as you couldn't get out.

I didn't ask her why she was there, but as I got to know her, she became my saviour; she was so funny and always made me laugh. She made comments about other people, like she shouldn't be there and that everyone else was a nutter and she wasn't. I later found out she had a drug issue and was being treated for that. What drug, I don't know, but I found that lots of people there were ice addicts, and some were scary to say the least.

Three times a day medication was given to all patients near the nurses' station, in a little room where the door's top section would open and the nurse stood behind it and dispensed the medication. There would usually be a line of people waiting before it even opened, and I remember one who yelled at the nurse while banging on the door saying, 'Give me my bloody drugs.' She was one scary woman, and I did everything possible to avoid her. She was staying in a room down the end of the hall of the women's section. Luckily, she kept to herself and stayed in her room most of the time; she rarely even came into the lounge area.

My sister had let my son know where I was plus my mum, dad and my brother. As I didn't have my mobile phone, all calls had to be made in the common area on a wall phone near the nurses' station. It was hard to make a call and certainly wasn't private. The calls had to be short, or you would end up having someone yell at you to get off. When on the phone I'd lean up against a wall with my finger in one ear while trying to talk quietly. It did feel like I was in prison and being on the phone felt like I was in a scene from a movie.

The first person I spoke to was my son. He was wonderful and understood why I was there as he knew I was in a dark place. He visited me a couple of days later, and we were able to go into a private area and talk with no one listening. He was so concerned for me and just wanted me to get better. Due to taking Valium I don't really recall much of our conversation; all I knew was that he loved me. My parents visited and also a close friend but that was all. I spoke to my brother and sister over the phone and that was it. I didn't get in touch with anyone else.

I was there for about a week, and it felt like a very long week. It was a stressful environment, and I was largely surrounded by drug addicts. I understand that drug addicts have mental health issues (let's face it, I took drugs for a long time, but these people were on a whole other level than I ever was), but they were mixed in with patients who had schizophrenia or bipolar, which are completely different mental health issues. I was dealing with deep depression and anxiety, and it felt like the facility increased my anxiety. It looked to me like these patients were neglected as the staff were running around trying to control the addicts coming off their drugs, who were often very aggressive. In the time I was there I only saw a doctor once and that was it, and I was there for about three days before I was assessed. I never had another doctor see me or any therapy sessions.

I give a great deal of credit to the nurses looking after these patients as it was clearly stressful having to deal with the aggressive people, and it was obvious they were understaffed.

As I was one of the quiet ones, I was questioned about going to another facility that was much more lowkey, and where I would probably get more help. I found that interesting as I was supposed to get help where I was staying, but all it did was make my anxiety go up; thank God I was being fed Valium. As I wasn't someone who had a drug dependence, I was interviewed via Zoom by the clinical psychologist at the facility and I was accepted. It was a ten-bed facility that was part of an old nursing home that had been shut down. You could leave and go for walks or to the shops and that is why drug addicts weren't allowed. Some of the people there had been in a psych ward and were in transition to going home, and this place helped them adjust back to 'normal' life.

It was much better for me there as you were able to talk to the clinical psychologists and have private discussions, plus I could learn ways of moving forward with my depression. We would also have group sessions and you got to know the others who were staying there. It was such a mixed bag of people. One woman had psychological issues because she had been abused, another had obsessive compulsive disorder, and another was a man wanting to transition to a woman. An interesting bunch to say the least, but we were all well cared for, and the staff were great. I stayed for about ten days. I could have stayed longer but I wanted to get home and back into my own space.

A couple of days after I returned home, I went to see a clinical psychologist that was connected to the psychiatric hospital, and she did a follow-up session with me. She asked if I'd like to continue to see her, but I decided to go back and see my psychologist in Melbourne as she knew my background. I had started seeing her about six months after I left my husband and continued to see her for a while, even though I lived an hour and a half away from her clinic. She always helped me and gave good advice. Going over old ground was horrible as I had tried doing that with a local psychologist and it was truly awful. I also saw my GP on a monthly basis, so she could see how I was going with my anti-depressants.

After being in the psychiatric ward and returning home, I started to get tinnitus; a constant ringing in the ears. Here I was trying to get on top of my depression and the ringing in my ears was driving me bloody mad, or should I say madder. At first the doctor thought it might be my medication, but we altered my anti-depressants and nothing changed. I then had hearing tests and MRIs, but they couldn't find anything that could be causing the ringing.

I just had to deal with it.

I actually believe it had a lot to do with my anxiety as when I was anxious my tinnitus was worse. Sometimes it was like a warning bell going off in my head that things were getting on top of me, or I was in a social situation that I wasn't comfortable with. I was put on more medication to help me sleep and as soon as I woke up, the slight buzz I heard in the morning felt like a siren by the evening. The only thing that helped was alcohol. Of course, I didn't want to go down that road again, but it was bloody hard. Many nights I just couldn't help myself as the ringing was driving me mad and I just wanted a reprieve from it. I didn't drink as much as I used to, and I had stopped smoking completely, but I knew I could easily fall back into bad habits.

I then had to go on diazepam to calm me during the day. Sometimes I thought I was just replacing one drug (alcohol) with another drug (prescription medication) but getting pissed every night was not the answer.

When my doctor (who I saw when still living in Melbourne) had first recommended I go on anti-depressants, I didn't want to as I was a bit scared of them. My grandmother was on a lot of medication for her mental health issues (she had bipolar), and she always seemed like she was in a bit of a daze. Because of that, I decided they weren't for me. About two years later I started to take them as I knew my mood was low, and my doctor kept saying that she thought they would be good for me, so I caved. I wasn't on a high dose and, frankly, I really don't know if they helped. Maybe my dose needed to be higher, but I was putting on weight and didn't like it, so I kept taking the lower dose.

I had just kept 'moving on'.

So, if I wasn't seeing my psychologist, I was seeing my GP, then I was referred to a psychiatrist because Centrelink wanted more and more proof from doctors about my condition so I could stay on unemployment benefits. They had received years of documentation from my current and previous doctors, plus the report from the psychiatric hospital, but they were never satisfied. My mental illness didn't seem to exist as far as they were concerned.

Admitting to myself that I had severe mental health issues and the fact I had a family history of mental illness was just the first step, the next was dealing with government departments that didn't accept mental illness.

Chapter 20

Mental health ignored

Australia is considered the 'Lucky Country', and in many ways we are. We don't have a war going on like in some countries, so what are we doing wrong?

Mental health issues have increased so much in this country, and around the world, that the latest Productivity Commission 2020[14] report states that it costs the Australian economy approximately $43 to $51 billion (yes, that's right, *billions*) a year, plus an additional $130 billion per year in costs associated with diminished health and reduced life expectancy for those living with mental ill-health.

In addition, depression is the number one cause of non-fatal disability in Australia. This means that, on average, people with depression live with this disability for a higher number of years than people suffering from other non-fatal diseases, such as hearing loss and dementia. The World Health Organization estimates that depression will be the number one health concern in both the developed and developing nations by 2030.

So, you have to ask, 'Why is this happening?'

Australia is seen as a chilled-out place but going by our mental health statistics that is clearly not the case. Yes, we have a great standard of living with everything available to us, but how much of that is created by living in debt? The cost of living is out of

---

[14] https://www.pc.gov.au/_data/assets/pdf_file/0019/249040/sub629-mental-health.pdf

control, and we are currently twelfth on the list of most expensive countries to live in around the world. The cost of living in Australia has increased so much that most people find it difficult to keep their heads above water. Unfortunately, it is only getting worse.

I have lived in this country for 57 years and have seen so many things change. Obviously, technology has come a long way, but it's only made our lives busier and faster. Yes, we were chilled out, but not anymore. Everyone is running around like idiots trying to keep up with everything and everyone. Due to the cost of housing, it is almost impossible now for one parent to stay at home to look after their children. Then there is the added cost of paying for expensive childcare. Sometimes, it is just not worth having both parents work as one of the wages coming into the family is just paying for childcare costs. A lot of women keep working even if it's just to pay for childcare as they want to continue their career and taking time off impacts their future career aspirations.

When it comes to mobile phones, I think they're evil. Yes, they're convenient, but they have made our lives so much faster as everyone wants things done yesterday. In particular when it comes to work. Some companies expect you to be available 24/7. We never get a rest as the boss can always contact you. The pressure this puts on people is immense and many people don't feel that they can rest, even when they're on holiday. I have known some people to be threatened with losing their job if they can't be contacted.

Mobile phone addiction is rife and also addiction to social media. We all see those happy pictures posted to convince everyone that their life is fantastic. They are not going to show you pictures of them crying with their head in their hands and unable to stop sobbing because they don't have enough money to pay the mortgage, rent or put food on the table. We are also obsessed with image and are made to feel we are less of a person if we don't have the big house, the fancy car and go on extravagant holidays where most of the happy snaps come from.

So many people are running on empty just trying to keep up with life's challenges and daily struggles and are constantly exhausted. Admitting you have a problem, or you can't cope, is largely hidden in society. Many won't admit they have a problem because there is still a huge stigma with mental health issues. I really think they should call it 'brain health'. The word 'mental' conjures up images of someone in a straitjacket being shoved into a padded cell. One movie that comes to mind for me is *One Flew Over the Cuckoo's Nest* starring Jack Nicholson and the famous character of Nurse Ratched, played by Louise Fletcher.

Brain health is more aligned with other terms, such as physical health, heart health, gut health and so on. If you call it brain health, it's considered just another organ that you have to look after. Poor brain health impacts general health because, ultimately, we can't do anything if we're in a poor state of mind. Unlike heart health, we are able to get a transplant just like many organs including liver, lung, pancreas, stomach, the list goes on. But when it comes to the brain, sorry that cannot be replaced, and I doubt it ever will. Therefore, it's important we ensure our brain health is in order.

Having seen for myself the state of the mental health system in this country, I feel strongly that a lot has to change. Having a family history of mental illness (my grandmother was bipolar), in my case I strongly believe that it was my life and other influences that caused me to end up in a psychiatric unit.

My condition was finally diagnosed by a psychiatrist as chronic dysthymia, which is known as persistent depressive disorder. This is where sufferers may experience symptoms for many years before it is diagnosed, if diagnosis occurs at all. As a result, they may believe that depression is a part of their character, so they may not even discuss their symptoms with doctors, family members or friends.

In a fifteen-page assessment it was also noted that I had suffered trauma related to experiences at work and with the legal system, and I had a lack of trust, phobic anxiety and suicidal thoughts, leading to being unable to work and the need for more ongoing therapy.

The psychiatrist who diagnosed me was the one I was forced to see by the Department of Health and Human Services because I was on unemployment benefits. My doctor at the time was helping me to receive a disability pension. I was reluctant to go down this path as I didn't see myself as disabled; I wasn't in a wheelchair and unable to walk, talk and I didn't need help with my day-to-day living. We all have a view of 'disabled', and I was no different from most people when it came to this view. The fact was, being on unemployment benefits and being unable to work I was living on $554.40 a fortnight, yes that's $277.20 a week. I was fortunate that I owned my own home and didn't have to pay rent, but I still had to pay all the other bills like electricity, rates, house insurance, car registration and everything else. Just going to the supermarket to get food was a challenge, and I made sure I wasted nothing.

My doctor knew that going on a disability pension would mean a bit more money – $944.30 a fortnight (472.15 a week) – which would help me keep my head above water and therefore help with my depression and not having to be constantly seeing government agencies regarding finding work.

After my hospitalisation, I was unable to work or even apply for jobs due to my condition. I was advised to apply for the disability pension when I returned home.

I applied for the disability pension on 6th October 2016, but my first appointment at Centrelink to discuss this was not until 6th January 2017. The appointment went for an hour. It was with a male, which to be honest was the first time I'd spoken to a male at Centrelink. I actually felt uncomfortable speaking to him as all of my doctors were female, and I'd always preferred to speak to females about my health conditions. I wasn't given the opportunity to have a preference for this interview on my mental health condition.

During the one-hour appointment, I was emotional and stressed talking to someone I hadn't met before. He had all of my medical evidence (which was considerable) and he asked a lot of questions regarding my health as well as personal information about my life. Halfway through the appointment, he sat in his chair behind a desk with his hands on the back of his head and elbows pointed outwards. Having seen this type of posture by men on many occasions, I knew it was a position of dominance and intimidation. A totally inappropriate body position while interviewing anyone, let alone someone dealing with depression and anxiety. At the end of the appointment, he told me I would be fine in about a year and that my disability application would be rejected. I was a complete mess by this stage and totally distraught. The man who made this judgement on me in just one hour was qualified as an occupational therapist, not a psychiatrist or psychologist or anything close to having the same expertise in mental health. Just the way he handled my interview was, in itself, totally unprofessional.

When I'd received the detailed assessment from the appointment with the occupational therapist at Centrelink on 6th January 2017, it stated that my mental condition was permanent and that I probably only had a capacity of working up to seven hours a week, but my claim for disability was rejected.

After a couple of days and having spoken to my doctor about the appointment, she encouraged me to make a complaint to Centrelink and that I would like to be interviewed again and this time by a woman. I contacted Centrelink on numerous occasions regarding another review appointment, but I didn't get acknowledgement about this in writing until 31st May 2017; five months after my original appointment. I subsequently had a half-hour talk over the phone with a review officer a few days later.

On 16th June 2017, I received a letter from the Centrelink Review Officer stating that my condition did not meet the requirements under the Mental Health Functions table and that my rating was 0. Although this person was more qualified than the man I saw on 6th January 2017 – she had a Master of Public Health (MPH), BA-HSC and other qualifications – I never had a face-to-face appointment with her, and I only spoke to her over the phone for about half an hour. In the letter that was sent afterwards, I was informed that if I was unhappy with the decision, I should apply to have a review by the Administrative Appeals Tribunal (AAT). As I had never met with the person who had made this decision, I made a further appeal.

On 7th September 2017, I received a letter from Centrelink regarding my claim to review the decision by the AAT. At this stage, Centrelink had to provide the AAT all the information on my file, which included my medical evidence and information about all of my contact with Centrelink and the considerable amount of phone calls made. In fact, at one stage I was told by Centrelink that my file had been misplaced.

I was contacted by the AAT and further discussed my claim. Subsequently, on 17th November 2017, it was acknowledged by the AAT that I had an impairment rating of at least twenty points under the impairment table for my condition, and that I qualified for the disability pension.

I was so relieved that this was over and I could finally concentrate on getting better, but unfortunately that didn't happen.

On 15th December 2017, I received a letter from the Department of Health and Human Services litigation branch that they were appealing the decision made by the AAT. I found this to be mind-blowing. They were the ones who'd told me to appeal to the AAT and now they were appealing the AAT's decision. The litigation department had requested that I have an independent assessment by a psychiatrist that was recommended by the Department of Health and Human Services.

By this stage, which had been over a year since my first application, my condition had worsened considerably. I had considered just walking away from the claim as I felt it was all a waste of time and, more importantly, energy that I didn't have. I was informed by the litigation department that an appointment had been made on 22nd February 2018, with an independent psychiatrist to assess my health condition. She was located in Melbourne and, as I live an hour and half away, I asked if it was possible to see someone more local as going into the city was extremely stressful for me. The request was rejected.

So, on 22nd February 2018, I had my appointment with the psychiatrist; this lasted about an hour and a half. It was incredibly draining, but I was relieved that at least it was with a woman. She asked *a lot* of questions, and she was kind in asking if I needed a break. I felt comfortable with her even though I was convinced she would side with Centrelink seeing as she was appointed by them. I almost didn't go, thinking it would be a waste of time, but a friend of mine convinced me that I had come this far with my claim that I may as well see it out to the end.

Approximately two weeks after this appointment, I was contacted by the litigation department at Centrelink that my claim had finally been accepted for the disability pension, and that the AAT had requested I be back-paid from the original application date of 6th October 2016. This process had taken over a year and a half!

To say that I was shocked is an understatement as I was convinced my claim was going to be rejected and that my mental health condition, as far as the Department of Health and Human

Services was concerned, didn't exist, despite the medical evidence.

The psychiatrist I saw on 22nd February confirmed my condition in a fifteen-page document. It also confirmed that my condition was permanent and ongoing treatment was required.

For a year and a half, the Department had rejected all the medical evidence that had been provided by my GP, a psychologist, a psychiatrist and the information supplied by the hospital it'd been admitted to. They considered that my condition didn't exist, and these decisions came from people who were not qualified to make them. During the year and a half this had gone on, my condition had worsened considerably, not only due to the stress, but, more importantly, because I wasn't believed, despite the medical evidence.

Once this horrible process was over, I could finally concentrate on getting better, yes, finally. I completely understand why people give up on their claims. I also believe strongly that the Department deliberately makes it hard so that people do give up. It is ultimately a government decision to reduce any type of welfare payment, at all cost!

With regard to mental health issues, it became obvious that the Department of Human Services could only identify a 'disability' as someone who had a physical disability and not a mental health disability. I was completely disregarded by Centrelink on my first appointment and by a person who had few qualifications and informed me that I would get better in a year. I was dismissed by every person I spoke to within the Department. They are meant to help people, but all they did was make my health worse.

When I look back on this time, I can't understand why they didn't do an assessment by their own psychiatrist at the beginning of my claim. Why did they keep on asking for more medical evidence, when all the existing evidence was continually dismissed? I can assure you that my own doctors were not impressed that their expertise and findings were being ignored.

I believe that when it comes to acknowledging mental illness, government departments need more training. It is well known that mental illness is stigmatised, and many people do not understand what it is like to have this type of condition. Often you are shunned by people, including family and friends, who don't know how to deal with it. I know, as I have had to deal with this myself.

The process is extremely harsh and unforgiving, and I imagine that many people would just give up, as I almost did.

As stated in the government's Productivity Report 2020[15], the key factors driving poor outcomes in Australia's mental health systems are:

> *Difficulties in finding and accessing*
> *suitable support, sometimes because the*
> *relevant services do not exist in regions*
> *where people need them.*

---

[15] https://www.pc.gov.au/research/ongoing/report-on-government-services/2020

Stigma and discrimination from family and friends is one thing, but where I suffered from the most was government departments. It is obvious that the system is broken. With departments not speaking to one another, and so many other organisations out there trying to help, it has all become a bad jigsaw puzzle with lots of pieces missing. The system needs to be more streamlined and, more importantly, it needs people with the qualifications to make decisions on medical conditions.

In the latest report by the Royal Commission into Victoria's Mental Health System[16], published in February 2021, it described the system as 'broken'. Despite the goodwill and hard work of many people, Victoria's mental health system has deteriorated for a multitude of reasons and over the course of many years. In November 2019, the Commission's interim report concluded that the system had catastrophically failed to live up to expectations and was underprepared for current and future challenges. Good mental health and wellbeing have been a low priority of governments at all levels and the community.

It also stated that reaching out for help and admitting you have mental health issues is hard enough in itself. I didn't like reaching out for help and, when I did, government departments pushed back at every turn to dismiss me.

Going through that difficult process to then be turned away makes the anxiety about reaching out even worse for fear of

---

[16] https://finalreport.rcvmhs.vic.gov.au/recommendations/

being told you aren't worthy of treatment. Turning people away because they 'aren't sick enough' sends a message that you have to get worse before you're allowed to get better.

Well, I certainly can relate to this as I was rejected again and again by the Department of Health and Human Services in relation to my mental health condition.

The reports on mental health by the federal and Victorian governments at least show that our leaders now see there is a major problem in society and not just because of COVID-19. The interim reports on mental health started well before we were hit by the pandemic.

The Productivity Commission report on Mental Health started taking submissions from the public back in 2019 and closed in January 2020 (just before the pandemic hit us) and was released to the public on 16th November 2020. These findings were damning of the current system, which is clearly failing. This report was timely considering COVID-19 was impacting everyone's mental health and particularly in Melbourne, which became the most locked down city in the world. The impact of these lockdowns will be felt for many years. At the time of writing this book, Melbourne has suffered through six lockdowns and more than 260 days under restrictions.

In late 2019 I decided to make a submission to the Productivity Commission report as I felt passionate about sharing my personal experience with mental health issues and accessing mental health services. It is a seventeen-page submission that you can read on the Productivity Commission's website[17]. A lot of what I have written about in this book is also in the submission, and also what reforms I think should happen in this area.

Many organisations and individuals made submissions to this report, and as a result the government has budgeted substantially more money towards mental health; however, it is yet to be seen whether this money will be spent effectively.

So, what happens from here is yet to be seen. It's a similar situation in our aged care sector, where massive faults have been identified in the system and yet little has been done so far to improve them. Once again it was thanks to COVID-19 that these failings were brought to the forefront. It's hard to have faith in the relevant government organisations and departments, where the people are paid good money and yet they can't get their acts together. These are 'educated' people who have qualifications in specialised areas but, in my opinion, they continue to fuck it up. Again, and again and again.

Will it improve? I really hope so.

All of us have life events that can throw us into a spin, and how we deal with them can impact us for a long time. Sweeping things under the carpet and thinking everything will just get better on its own is not the way to deal with our mental health issues because they usually come back to haunt us. The reason we drink, smoke, take drugs and eat too much is usually to give us some form of comfort to cover up the pain.

---

[17] https://www.pc.gov.au/_data/assets/pdf_file/0019/249040/sub629-mental-health.pdf

As much as we all need to look after our health, it's easier said than done. Many people struggle with trying to keep fit and lose weight but return to old habits and put all the weight back on. Giving up alcohol, drugs and smoking are major battles for millions around the world. I have battled all three and I can assure you that not relying on these things makes you a lot happier. You think at first you won't be able to cope without them and you convince yourself you deserve to feel good. Aussies love a drink and largely that is accepted in this country when really it is a major problem, not just for our health but also because of the violence it leads to.

I still love a drink when catching up with friends and having a great meal. I really don't think I could give it up completely, and nor should I, if my health is okay. On a recent liver test, I was as good as gold. I have often thought that the liver is a resilient organ and has the greatest regenerative capacity of any organ in the body. If you overdo it, your liver will most definitely fail you, but giving your liver a rest from alcohol, even short term, can have great benefits. I don't miss smoking at all. Or the waking up in the morning coughing.

When it comes to over-eating, many are guilty of it and obesity is out of control around the world. I was never really overweight until I got to my forties. Drinking too much gained the weight for me, and now that I'm in my fifties, it is hard to get that weight off. All of these things contribute to our health, and over-indulgence only makes things worse when it comes to our mental health.

I'm not suggesting giving up everything as that is just unrealistic for most people. We all want pleasures in life, and this is a natural human desire. Life is short and I want to live as long as I can and be able to do all the things that living life can bring. To do that, you need to look after your mind, and if you do that your body will follow and lead you into a healthier lifestyle without just living on celery and water.

I give myself credit for digging myself out of the dark hole and managing, most of the time, to stay near the top, but I still work at keeping my mental health on track. It is not an easy path, but it is a path you can choose to take. You can get your life back on track, and it could be a far better life than you could have ever expected it to be.

I thought moving away from Melbourne would take away the pain of the end of my marriage, leaving my son and losing friends, but all I did was take it with me. You can't run away from pain and hope it doesn't catch up to you. Instead, you have to walk through the fire and try to be strong enough to get to the other side. That is what I learnt along the way from trying to hide the hurt and bury it in the earth, only to have it rise up again. The moment you realise you can't keep burying what you feel is when you start to heal.

Instead of companies and governments spending *lots* of money on conferences and junkets, they should be 'brain health retreats', which focus on having more respect for yourself and the people you work with. If you care for yourself and others, not only in the workplace but also outside the workplace, then it is only a natural progression that everyone's mental health will be better. Greed in all forms, whether it is corporate greed or personal greed, is killing our society and it needs to stop.

Some people still seem to think all this mental health stuff is bullshit, but I don't believe it is. They will find out one day when something really bad happens and they're in a position where they are so unhappy it's hard to 'move on'.

I hope COVID-19 has helped the world open its eyes and see what is going on. We are all hell-bent on having everything and being the best and the richest with the nicest car. That all means nothing when you can't drive your car, have friends or family over for dinner and the only reason you can get out of the house is for essential reasons. Possessions are nothing if you don't have your health.

Many people are horrible to one another in families too; nastiness is not exclusive to the workplace. The difference is that in the workplace, the people who you spend most of your day with have no idea what is really going on in your life when you leave for the day. As the saying goes, 'You never know what is going on behind closed doors.'

I wish we could all become kinder and more considerate of other people's feelings. Life is hard, and yes there are good times, but for most, life is not always easy. We all have challenges we have to overcome, it's just that some have more challenges than they can deal with.

Close to 800,000 people die because of suicide every year around the world, and many more attempt to take their own lives, according to data from the World Health Organization[18]. In many countries, suicide is morally considered a sin and therefore it isn't reported. The fact that in some countries it is hidden only

---

[18] https://www.who.int/news-room/fact-sheets/detail/suicide

proves that many people do not like to talk about how sad they feel, or that they just don't want to live in this world anymore.

Nine Australians die every day by suicide. That's more than double the road toll. The sad facts are these:

1. 75 percent of those who take their own life are male.
2. Over 65,000 Australians make a suicide attempt each year.
3. In 2019, 3,318 Australians took their own lives.
4. Suicide is the leading cause of death for Australians between the ages of 15 and 44.

It is interesting to see that men are more likely to take their own lives than women. Research shows that men are less likely to seek support for mental health issues and are less likely to disclose a mental health problem to friends or family. Having known many men in my life, it largely comes down to pride. Men don't want to be seen as weak and unable to cope, which I find really sad. Men need to open up and be honest about their feelings, which the large majority of men see as being something a woman does. Obviously, men have a lot to learn from women when it comes to this.

I admit that I hid my sadness too. I didn't want people to know that I wasn't in a good place when it came to my thoughts. When I look back now, I can see that most of my depression came from the workplace through bullying, sexual harassment and discrimination. There is no doubt that losing a job can cause depression, particularly when you don't see it coming, and also when you can't understand why you are dismissed. Coming back from something like that is not easy. People say, 'You'll get another job,' but the reality is that trying to find another job is not easy and the process of sending résumés and going for interviews is a gruelling process even for confident people.

My road to recovery has been a long one and something I have to work on every day. Many things can impact your mental health and 'moving on' in life can be so difficult that many simply can't and sadly take their own lives.

Much is spoken about now when it comes to our mental health and many people disregard it and say that people use it as an excuse for not being themselves or they see that person as unable to deal with day-to-day life. We have to ask ourselves why mental health issues are on the increase and why so many people are taking their own lives?

Chapter 21

The turning point

On 14th May 2019, it was six years to the day since I'd left my husband. I had come a long way and felt like a different person. A much happier one, finally, is the first thing that comes to mind. I had just come back from a yoga and meditation retreat on Magnetic Island. It would have to be, without a doubt, one of the best things I've done in the past six years.

I had been looking at going away to some type of retreat. I'd been on holiday a couple of times since leaving my husband. I did a trip to Cairns on my own for a couple of weeks when our family house had been sold and the settlement money had come through. I was living with my parents at the time, and they were a bit worried about me being on my own. The reality was that I had felt alone for a long time already, so going away alone was no different, except I'd be in a warm place and staying in a nice hotel. I could sit by the pool and drink cocktails and try not to think about my life too much.

The next time I went away on my own was to the Northern Territory, and I ticked three things off my bucket list: seeing Uluru, going on The Ghan and staying in Darwin. It was a wonderful trip and one that will stay in the box of good memories for a long time. But at this time, I needed more from a trip away, a bit more soul-searching and looking after my mind and body at the same time.

Having been through so much to get my life back on track, I knew I had to continue to do the work to look after myself. Even to this day I still say, 'I am a work in progress' and will need to continue to work on keeping myself well. I don't want to just rely on anti-depressants for the rest of my life as they really just push your feelings down.

I did go on a two-night retreat with a new friend I'd met in the area, and we stayed at the Gawler Foundation in the Yarra Valley for a meditation retreat. Harpist Michael Johnson was running the retreat and my friend loved to listen to him. I had done some meditation one on one with a local lady in the area, and she was wonderful in helping me learn about meditation. It's not something you can do at the click of a finger. Just like most things that you haven't done before, it takes practice to become good at it. Going to the Gawler Foundation helped me enhance my meditation experience, but I was more than aware I needed more help in dealing with my depression.

I did a Google search to try to find something that would fit my needs, and I came across a lot of retreats that incorporated yoga and meditation. I also looked at rehabilitation retreats but most of them were so expensive they almost blew me off my chair when I saw the price. Some of these places were charging $10,000 for one week. *Ouch!* That was way out of my budget and frankly I thought most of them looked like a complete rip-off.

The sad reality is that most people with addictions or mental health issues don't have $10,000 for a luxury stay at a rehab for a week. I actually don't think a week is long enough for most people anyway because if you have these types of conditions it takes a long time to get back on track. After you leave a rehab facility is when the hard work starts. They can set you on a path though and give you the information you need to get better, but the direction you take is ultimately up to you.

I was in the position of being able to go away on a whim as I wasn't working at the time. I was also fortunate enough to have some money in my bank account. Using some of it to improve my health was what I considered a good investment.

A retreat popped up at Magnetic Island. It was with a small group of women, some shared rooms but they also had rooms where you had your own bathroom. The retreat included all your food for four days, and yoga and meditation were plentiful. As it was heavily discounted, I thought, 'I'm booking it,' and before I knew it, I was booking flights for the following week to Townsville. I had never booked a holiday so quickly in my life. Maybe Magnetic Island was pulling me in, just like a magnet.

When viewing the accommodation online the rooms looked lovely, and one in particular was a stunning room overlooking Horseshoe Bay. I thought it would be wonderful to have that room and assumed it was already taken as I was the last one to book the retreat. On my arrival, I was picked up from the harbour by a man called Alex and driven to the accommodation that was on the other side of the island. When I got to the house, I thought it was lovely. A two-storey property with a pool and a veranda that overlooked the bay. Alex helped me with my bags, and we started to walk over to another property that was next door. He told me that both properties had been booked for the retreat and I would be staying in the house next door.

We entered the house through some beautiful Balinese doors, then went up the staircase to the main level, where there was an expansive lounge and kitchen area. Two bedrooms were on that level, and I assumed one of them was my room. As I followed, Alex was taking my bags out to the veranda, which was filled with Balinese furniture and the view was beautiful. I was thinking, *Why the hell is he taking my luggage onto the veranda?* We then went to a set of stairs at the side of the veranda, and he lugged my suitcase up the wooden staircase. I said, 'Where are you taking me?' He said that I had the 'special room', and that the others were very jealous. As I entered the room, I was absolutely gobsmacked.

Alex smiled at me and said, 'I'm jealous too!'

The group of ladies at the retreat fondly referred to my room as the 'Princess Suite'. It was the room I'd seen on Google when booking, but I never thought in a million years I would be staying in it. It had two large sliding doors that opened onto a veranda, the biggest bed I had ever slept in and a massive walk-in wardrobe and a luxurious bathroom. I couldn't believe my luck; it was just meant to be, and I felt that the universe was finally being kind to me.

Alex left the room and said that everyone would be meeting at the other house for a meet and greet. I unpacked a few things and settled in. I stood on the balcony and admired the magnificent view. When walking back down the stairs I noticed I overlooked a lovely pond with a little fountain. It was so peaceful and serene, just what I needed. I met the other people on the retreat, they were all women, twelve in total plus three people who organised all the walks, yoga and meditation, and our wonderful cook.

When being introduced everyone said, 'Oh, you're Linda, the one who got the best room.' I felt a bit embarrassed at first, but they were all saying how glorious the room was as they had all taken a sticky beak before I arrived.

I saw it as a sign that the universe was rewarding me for all my efforts to get my life back on track.

The next few days were a turning point for me as this retreat taught me about spending time looking after myself, being able to slow down my mind and doing some reflection on my life and how far I had come. Before the retreat I was still drinking too much, even though I'd cut down considerably I knew I still had old habits to break. I didn't smoke marijuana anymore, but I still enjoyed the occasional cigarette, which was also a habit from my youth, but it was something I stopped completely after the retreat.

Even though you were allowed to drink alcohol, I didn't indulge too much as I was up early doing yoga. I purchased a bottle of wine and that lasted me the entire time. I only had a glass of wine with dinner and, even then, I felt guilty about it as I'd promised myself I wouldn't drink on the retreat. It's funny how you're influenced by others when it comes to drinking. We have such a massive drinking culture in Australia and many people who don't drink are seen as being a bit strange. I think, *More power to you.*

Even though I'm a good cook, I can be judgemental when it comes to food, particularly when eating out. I hate paying a lot of money for food at a restaurant that's a bit average and I could have done better, but when it came to the food on the retreat, it was wonderful. It was mainly vegetarian, and I don't think there was one thing I didn't like. The cook was amazing, not just with the food but her personality was as well. It was a hard gig having to feed all of us. I don't know if many appreciate the hard work that goes into cooking and preparing that amount of food every day – three meals a day – and we were never hungry. Having cooked for other people with my business in Melbourne, I know how hard it is. Standing all day in the kitchen working up a sweat can be exhausting. I managed to have a couple of chats with the cook while she was preparing things and she was such a beautiful soul.

First thing in the morning we would go for a silent walk along the beach. I loved that, as sometimes talking just takes up too much energy. Some found this a bit difficult but I never did. Just talking chitter-chatter while walking doesn't allow you to just take in the scenery and the sounds of the waves crashing on the beach. On our return we would meditate by the pool, and all you could hear were the waves and the birds. As both houses were at the end of the main street along the beach, you rarely heard cars so it felt rather secluded. We would then have breakfast and do some yoga and after that we had some free time to look around the island. We would all return for lunch and hang by the pool, read a book or have a massage. Later we would do yoga again and then return for dinner.

I recall on the second night when we did yoga in a large lounge area that opened up onto the balcony. I took up a space on the floor in the balcony area as it was more than warm enough to go outside. The yoga sessions went for an hour and a half as it was a much slower version of yoga and you stayed in the positions for up to five minutes. At one stage I was lying on my back, and I could look up and see the dark sky and the moon was almost full. The stars were shining and it was simply beautiful. It was a powerful moment as I felt at peace with the world and lucky to be alive and well; a very different place than two years before when I wanted to end it all.

On the last day, everyone was leaving at different times due to their flights, but I was in no hurry to leave as I was spending another two days in Townsville to have a bit of a look around. The fact was, I hadn't even booked my flight home yet. I had never done anything like that before when going on holiday; I always had a flight booked to get back home but, on this occasion, I was winging it.

As there were only about five of us left on the retreat and staying for lunch, we indulged in a non-vegetarian treat of local prawns, and then later I took a drive with Alex to Arcadia Bay, which was another beach on the east side of the island. There was a small market and I purchased a memento to take home with me. It was a bracelet made of oyster shells, and it's something I wear a lot as it always reminds me of my time on Magnetic Island. Later that day the rest of us were taken to the ferry by Alex and we all said our goodbyes. Little did I know that it would not be the last time I would see Alex.

For the next couple of days, I checked out Townsville and booked my flight home. It was a late flight leaving at 11.30pm and I thought it would be horrible as I would be getting back to Melbourne at about 4am. I got onto the plane, sat down in my window seat and watched as the people poured onto the plane. I had two seats next to me and as the people came down the aisle, I kept hoping that only one seat would be taken, and we could have space between us. Suddenly, the doors were being shut, I looked to see if any more people were coming down the aisle and everyone was seated. The plane was almost full bar a couple of seats, and they were both next to me. I couldn't believe my luck.

When the plane took off, I pulled up the side arms in between the seats and got my little pillow out and had a nap lying down –

what a win. The universe was looking over me again. I woke up about half an hour before landing and felt great and ready for the drive back to my little seaside home. That had never happened to me before.

I never considered myself a lucky person, but this holiday was meant to be and luck followed me all the way.

Following the retreat, I finally gave up the smokes and never looked back. I was done with them and when I smell smoke now it just reminds me that I never want to go back to that bad habit. As for drinking, well, I still drink but my intake keeps on decreasing and I now actually have AFDs (alcohol free days). To think I was drinking a bottle of wine a day, sometimes more. I still love having a good wine with a meal, and I like to have a nice cold beer on a warm day. I find wine goes to my head really quickly now, and I wonder how I managed to function at all when I drank a lot. Your body adapts when drinking or taking drugs though; the more you have the more you need to numb the pain, and getting off the spiral is hard.

Retreats should be compulsory; they are an opportunity to look within. Some people would hate the thought of 'retreat' and think it's boring but the fact is, your body needs to slow down so it can repair.

I can't recommend them enough if you're having difficulties in your life. Even if you think everything is okay, I have no doubt that a retreat will be of benefit to give you some clarity and direction in your life. You may not be into yoga and meditation but when you give them a go, they will undoubtedly give your mind and body benefits that will improve your life. They have helped me in so many ways.

You can do anything you like when it comes to some form of retreat, but the most important thing is to slow down and finally smell the roses and stop being caught up in the rat race. We all need time out, but many don't and unfortunately that is why I believe mental health is in crisis around the world.

So, do yourself a favour and go somewhere to slow down and breathe.

Chapter 22

Airy fairy bullshit

For a long time, wellness retreats, meditation and yoga weren't on most people's radar when it came to the benefits they can have for your health. Wellness tourism is massive now all around the world. People want to come back from their time away as a new, improved, better version of themselves.

When I say 'airy fairy bullshit', I know that is what a lot of people say when it comes to these types of activities because I said it myself. I started yoga about twenty years ago and found that some of the classes I went to were not that good, but then I came across a great teacher, and that is when I changed my mind. I did it on and off for many years but fell off the wagon a couple of years before my marriage ended. I finally started it up again when I moved and slowly got back into it. Now, I try to do it at least twice a week and find when I don't, my body seems to crack up.

When it came to self-help books, I also thought they were, well, airy fairy bullshit, but one day when I was out walking with a friend, she suggested we go past the library. The library I knew of was about three kilometres away, and I wasn't going to walk that far in the hot weather. But this little library was just around the corner, and you could take books from it or place books you have read into it.

It was a small cupboard in the front yard of a house. It had about three shelves with a glass door. We stopped and had a look. 'You might find something you'd like to read,' my friend said. I didn't read much but I had a look anyway and picked up *Light is the New Black* by Rebecca Campbell. I was still at a stage in my life where I was trying to 'find myself'. I used to think this was a cheesy saying but it is the only words I can think of that refers to where I was in my life.

I was in Melbourne staying with my friend for a couple of days but when I finally went home and started to read the book, I couldn't put it down. It resonated with me on so many levels. It made me look at myself and think about what I wanted in life. It was the type of book I wouldn't have purchased because it was about your soul calling you to a new direction and to uncover what lights you up. I never felt that my life had much direction, and when I did think I was on the right path something came along to push me off it.

When I told my friend that I had already read the book from the little library, and I really enjoyed it she said, 'You were meant to have that book.' She was right.

I did feel that I was on the wrong path when it came to my life, and reading this book helped me think more about what I wanted to do. So, it set me on a path to believing in myself again, and that I had something to offer in this crazy world we live in.

For the next few months, I read some other books my friend gave me. She's well-read and knew that reading was a great way to escape and stop you from thinking about other shit in your head. The next few books I read were mainly fiction; it was an escape from thinking about my life, but when I finished a book my own reality came back. It's hard to forget the horrible things that have happened in your life, but I was trying hard to not let them control me anymore.

For many years I hid how I really felt and faked it a lot. So much had happened and sometimes I used to write about my struggles. My psychiatrist told me that writing things down can be great therapy. I found that when I did write, it helped me get the crap out of my head. I would put it down on paper and it didn't spin around in my head as much. I could look back and read it months later and see what I was thinking and maybe add to it. Before I knew it, I had written a great deal about my life and struggles. I used to imagine writing a book and getting it published and hoping that it would help other people realise that they are not alone.

I was on my computer one day and looking up Rebecca Campbell as I wanted to see if she had any other books I could read. That is when I discovered Hay House. I went to their site and saw that they were having a writers' workshop in Melbourne that July. Naturally, it was about writing a book, but one of the guest speakers was Rebecca Campbell. I thought to myself, I must meet this woman. I also thought that it would be interesting to learn about writing, even though I never really thought I could do it.

The workshop went for two days, and I stayed in an apartment just nearby. It was a lovely weekend staying in the city and the weather was also kind to me considering it was the middle of winter.

I was surprised by the amount of people there. About three hundred, I would guess, maybe more. It was in a big auditorium. I met a lot of interesting people and they all wanted to write, some about health issues, others about life experiences and many self-help types of books. The one person I was looking forward to listening to was Rebecca. I was just interested in knowing what type of person she was. I know you don't get to know someone from just listening to them on stage, but it was more about what she might say.

Many people were there to see her, and when there was a break, she was doing book signings, but the line was always about 50–60 deep. I thought I would get nothing signed by her.

When she finally got on stage, she was so upbeat, had a lot of energy and she was always smiling. She made you feel like you could do anything and that all you had to do was put your mind to it and never doubt yourself. At the end of her talk, she asked people to come onto the stage. I went up; something I would never normally do. A song came on, it was John Farnham's 'You're the Voice'. She made us all sing and dance on the stage. The rest of the audience sang along as well. It was a laugh and I'm glad I went on stage. I doubted myself so much. That's why I really loved her book, *Light is the New Black*; it's so positive and makes you believe you can do anything.

During the two days, many people asked questions about book writing and other writers spoke about their journey of writing their books. All of them said they questioned themselves whether their story was worth writing about, or if anyone would read it. I was no different from anyone else in the room. I questioned whether my story was worth the read too.

When speaking to one of the women there, we talked about what type of book we were going to write. She wanted to write about her job in psychiatry, and I told her I wanted to write about my experiences in the workplace, and that I was the first woman to go to court for unfair dismissal while being on maternity leave. She was blown away; I am always surprised when people react like that. She said it would be interesting reading. The fact she said this to me made me think that my story was worth telling and it gave me the confidence to start writing this book.

At the lunchbreak Rebecca Campbell was still signing books and also signing her oracle cards. The line wasn't as long so I thought that this was the time to get something signed. I wanted her to sign my Hay House workshop book as I thought it would give me a good vibe. As I stood in front of her, she turned over the next oracle card to sign and all it said was 'Yes'. She looked at me and smiled and said, 'Well, that tells you all you need to know; not many of those cards have come up.' She signed it and allowed me to take a picture of the two of us so that I captured the moment I met her. I know it might seem silly to rely on an oracle card that said 'Yes', but it was the push I needed to write. I have this card on the wall above where my computer sits, and it reminded me to complete my book.

I then purchased her new book, *Rise Sister Rise*, as well as Louise Hay's *You Can Heal Your Life*, Elizabeth Peru's *Cosmic Messengers* and Bronnie Ware's *The Top Five Regrets of the Dying*. I read them all in about four weeks, which is outstanding for me as sometimes I can sit on books for months and forget what I've read about. I loved *The Top Five Regrets of the Dying* and reading it at top speed – two days – I couldn't put it down. This book made me realise about the many regrets that people live with, and it made me more determined to do more with my life.

I sometimes wonder where the years have gone, not unlike many people, but I didn't want to continue to have my depression control my life. I felt I had more to offer and telling my story felt like the right thing to do.

At first, I thought that by putting myself out there and telling my story, many people I know would be shocked at how unwell I had become in my life. Many people judged me for leaving my son behind and I hope that if they get the opportunity to read this book, they will understand more about why I made the decisions I did.

I have tried hard in my life not to upset others and do the 'right thing', but in doing that, all I did was make them feel good and not look after myself. I neglected myself so much and just pushed through. I guess a lot of people do that because they feel good about helping someone. Nothing wrong with that but now I know that you can't really help others unless you also look after yourself.

You also have to surround yourself with likeminded people and let go of the ones who bring negativity into your life; they are just not worth it. It is not an easy thing to do, and you may have been good friends (or so you thought) for a long time. Letting go of someone hurts you as well. You wish things were different and you could still be friends, but as we get older, we do change. What has happened in your life and how you deal with those events will make you the person you are today. A lot of what occurs in our lives is out of our control and we have no idea what is to come in the future. You can make the best laid-out plans, but someone or something can come along and pull the rug from underneath you and everything changes.

You can only plan your life to a certain degree, like where you might live, if you want to study to be a doctor, if you want to travel… but when it comes to the people who cross our paths in life, you have no control over that. Some people you might take a dislike to straight away and others you think are nice, funny, social and just great to be around. Some want to be your friend, but you really don't want to be theirs, and that can be a tricky minefield. With so many personalities in the world you simply can't get along with everyone, it's just not possible.

I consider myself a trusting person and sadly that has gotten me hurt. I would not be the first, or the last, person on this earth to trust and be hurt, and sometimes it takes a while before you can see what a person is really like. Once you lose trust, it's hard to let that person in your life again.

Writing this book gave me the opportunity to think back on the things that have happened in my life, and now I can see that I've been very resilient. To be knocked down so many times and manage to get back up again took strength. But when you've been knocked down a lot, you do question yourself on what type of person you are.

I knew I was considered friendly, loved a good laugh and generally got along with most people. I most definitely became a more resilient person, but I guess as you get older you think you are more resilient because of life experiences and lessons learnt. Maybe you just become wiser.

I would like to think I have become wiser. In saying that, my mother said often, *If only I knew the things I know now when I was younger*. Now that I'm older, I understand what she was talking about.

Life is about constantly learning, and no matter how old we are we all have lessons to learn. You can be taught lessons in life but until you actually experience all the twists and turns, it is only then the lessons are learnt.

I absolutely believe that I'm a good person and that my heart is always in the right place. I really hate seeing people treated badly and that you can't always judge a book by its cover. I know that over the years patience was not my strong point as I hate it when people are late or when you have to wait in a long queue.

We all see ourselves differently to how others see us. Over the years I did put on a brave face and tried to brush things off, but unlike many other people who just say, 'move on' or 'let it go', I found that difficult to do. I do work hard on not letting things get to me as much as I used to.

We all have a process to go through when it comes to dealing with pain and hurt, and for some it takes longer. Some may never truly get past the pain and just learn to live with it.

Being in predominantly sales and customer service positions, my personality came out and my naturally talkative nature came out even more. I learnt to read people fairly well and particularly in a face-to-face sales environment. When it came to my facial expressions, that is where I got into trouble. I tried hard over the years not to have facial reactions, but it was a hard trait to control. Sometimes when I was deep in thought, or I didn't react, people would ask me if I was okay because I wasn't my usual chatty self.

I know I was caught doing the eye-roll, but it was usually when a man made an inappropriate comment. My face gave me away and it still does today. I have been told on many occasions that I'm really expressive when I tell a story. I don't even realise I'm doing it, so I guess that is just my personality.

I'm guilty of having a short fuse, but if something is fundamentally wrong it makes me angry. Some people call it being passionate.

I have found that women who are passionate come across strong in a discussion. They are seen differently to a man who does the same thing. As much as I come across as fairly confident, it hides behind a lack of confidence that few have seen.

I have tried to figure out over the years if I have brought all of the things that happened onto myself because of the way I behave or speak. Some I probably have because I didn't have the patience to deal with people who were rude to me, but then why should I be nice to someone who is rude to me? Walk away, others will say, and just cop it on the chin, particularly in sales because you have a budget forecast to achieve. Believe me, I dealt with some rude people over the years, and I copped it on the chin for the sake of the sale on many occasions.

A woman having confidence in a male-dominated workplace does not always come off as a good thing. As much as this has shifted over the years, the comment, 'she's got balls' is still a common phrase.

I did speak up sometimes in meetings and give my point of view, but I was never really listened to, and over the years I became more reluctant to say anything, particularly when it was a meeting full of men.

I recently spoke to an old colleague about what he thought I was like at work. He told me that he knew if he asked me to do something at work, he could rely on me to get the job done. He knew I was good at sales and that I was great at dealing with clients. I stood up for myself and that didn't go well with management. I wasn't a 'yes' person, which is what a lot of management like. Even he said that with a lot of companies people who aren't 'yes' people and question management decisions are often the ones who are let go because they don't toe the line or they're considered not a 'team player', which was most certainly the case with my unfair dismissal claim. I was considered a top salesperson and made money for the company, but that wasn't taken into consideration when they made me redundant. I did come across as confident, but you had to be, particularly in a sales position. I do think that many men still find confident women intimidating and they don't know how to deal with it.

Even though most of the sexual harassment I endured was in the '80s and '90s, and it was far more blatant that it is today, I always held my ground and tried not to be intimidated by it. I would be seen doing an eye-roll or the one eyebrow raised as if to say, *Really!*

Now more than ever we are encouraged to stand up and call out people's offensive comments or behaviour, but women still have to be careful of how they do this. Adverts for men calling out other men's behaviour have been encouraged but we still have a long way to go with that as even men are reluctant to do this for fear of being ridiculed.

We all walk along a tightrope when it comes to standing up to how other people behave. It could go either way – it could stop a bad situation from getting worse or you could accelerate it. I completely understand why people walk away and say nothing.

The world is a hard place to navigate, and sometimes you do have to be careful, but if we all walked away when something was wrong then the bullies of the world would rule, and that is something I wouldn't want to see. I stood up to bullies in the workplace and that was to my detriment.

In my last full-time job, I did all of the appropriate things you need to do when needing assistance at work and followed the 'rules', but because I chose to speak up and say I wasn't being trained properly it was the demise of my job and the main reason why I was dismissed. I spoke out about how I was being treated, and instead of the company dealing with these issues it was easier to sack me instead of fixing the real problems.

Even when it came to family, I hated it when we had arguments. For a number of years my family had to overcome a difficult split that had occurred and it caused a lot of pain for all of us. This situation would not have been fixed if it wasn't for me stepping up and facing it head on. I was not prepared to have this horrible situation continue for years and years when all that was needed was a frank discussion and for all of us to see that not dealing with it and facing up to what was really going on was not working for any of us.

I tried to convince my family on many occasions that we had to try to fix it, but I was constantly told that it wouldn't work because of outside influences and other people who wanted to hide the truth about what was really going on. When the truth came out about some money issues, everything started to fall into place and our family reconnected back to the way it should be. Instead of listening to others I went out on a limb and confronted the situation head on, and I really didn't know which way it would go, but it all worked out for the benefit of everyone in my family.

As Oprah Winfrey has said on many occasions, 'The truth will set you free.'

I can assure you it does.

Chapter 23

Women finding themselves

I never thought when I was growing up that because I was born a girl, my life would be much harder than it was for boys. When I was born in the '60s a lot was changing, women were burning their bras, going on the pill to stop unwanted pregnancies and in general pushing for more rights and equality.

As a young girl in the '70s I never really gave it much thought about what I would do when I became an adult. I knew I would probably work in an office like my mum had. I did think about hairdressing, but it was just because other girls wanted to do that. I really don't ever recall being encouraged to do anything. Having a job in a male-dominated arena was something I just didn't consider.

It was only 1978 when women were legally allowed to work beside men in the police force doing the same duties, and even today only 19 percent of women are in active duty.[19]

The Equal Opportunity Act *was implemented within Victoria Police in 1978. It also removed the marriage bar (married women were able to join, and single women were able to remain after marriage). Women were to receive the same training (including self-defence and pistol training) and were officially able to carry handcuffs, batons and guns.*

---

[19] https://www.police.vic.gov.au/100-years-women-policing

As I mentioned earlier in this book, when you google famous women from the '70s there were few in powerful positions. I can't recall any.

Today there are so many more female role-models, in sports, as company CEOs and many others, but even when you google this in 2021 it still largely consists of women in mainstream media positions or actresses. I love Oprah Winfrey because she is a self-made woman. She has come from humble beginnings to become an influential woman of the world who gives a large portion of her wealth to charities. She encourages wellness of mind, body and spirit and advocates mental health awareness and the importance of looking after yourself both mentally and physically.

It seems there is still a long way to go before women get a fair go in politics. Political journalist Annabel Crabb investigated the experience of women in parliament, from early struggles for the most basic of facilities, such as toilets to the persistent problems of harassment. *Ms Represented* aired in 2021, and she interviewed past and present women in politics and the difficulties they had to endure being in a male-dominated arena.[20]

I admire all of the women on this show as it would have taken a great deal of strength to go into politics and have to deal with the discrimination and harassment and also have to follow the party line to be able to keep their positions.

Around the world more women are going into politics, and there have been successes like Kamala Harris – the first South Asian-

---

[20] https://iview.abc.net.au/show/ms-represented-with-annabel-crabb

American to become US vice-president – and Jacinda Ardern, the Prime Minister of New Zealand. Fantastic role-models, but they would have, without a shadow of doubt, had great challenges achieving their goals in a male-dominated arena.

One woman I admire greatly is Rosie Batty. After her son Luke was tragically murdered by her husband, she has dedicated her life to campaigning against domestic violence. In 2015 she became Australian of the Year and through her own tragedy she put a spotlight on domestic violence in Australia and around the world:

- *On average, one woman a week is murdered by her current or former partner.*
- *1 in 3 Australian women (34.2%) has experienced physical and/or sexual violence perpetrated by a man since the age of 15.*[21]

Trying to find up-to-date statistics for rape and sexual assault in Australia is extremely difficult but it's suggested that one in twelve sexual assault reports are allegations that are groundless, where not enough evidence is available, and they're not investigated further and are subsequently thrown out. The large majority of women do not report assaults due to the gruelling process of reporting the crime to police and subsequently being portrayed as a slut in the courtroom. A report by the ABC reported alarming figures of how the police are failing survivors of sexual assault.[22]

---

[21] https://www.ourwatch.org.au/quick-facts/
[22] https://www.abc.net.au/news/2020-01-28/how-police-are-failing-survivors-of-sexual-assault/11871364?nw=0

I consider myself blessed to have been raised by a man who worked hard to put a roof over my head and food on the table, and I never saw him raise a hand to my mother. My parents are in their eighties and are still together today. I love the fact they are still independent and live active lives. My ex-husband never physically hurt me either, but I am more than aware that many women have abusive partners, and they are ashamed or petrified of speaking out.

Both my parents worked, which wasn't really the norm back in the '70s. Most of my friends had mothers who stayed at home looking after the kids. They may have had a part-time job but that was about it. I do recall my mother working part-time when I was really little, but by the time I was about halfway through primary school, she was working full-time as a secretary. I recall coming home from school, and if I was home first, I would get the key from the garage and go into the house. As I got older, I would help clean the breakfast dishes and tidy up the house a bit before my parents got home. I recall many arguments with my sister about who did more!

Don't get me wrong, I think the fact my mother worked full-time was fine. She contributed financially and enabled us to do things like camping over the Christmas school holidays, which I have fond memories of. Not many families in my suburb went away on camping holidays, so I guess I was one of the lucky ones who got to see a lot of Australia.

Today, women want more than just being a stay-at-home mother and doing all the housework, shopping and cooking and, of course, looking after the children. Trouble is, women today are working more than ever. Sadly, women are often still expected to be the homemaker and do most of the chores around the house and hold down a job. I'm not saying that it's like that in all households, but women are still doing most of the work around the house.

It saddens me greatly that women give so much of themselves to look after the family. Some will stay with their partner just to keep the family together, have a roof over their head and food on the table. Along the way, they can lose themselves trying to keep everyone happy. I know I did.

Most men want women to work and contribute financially to the family, plus have a career, but I think they still have a lot to learn when it comes to helping equally around the house. Housework is still seen as 'women's work'. Lots of men I know now and even men much younger than myself still have expectations that women will do most of the household chores. It's largely because that's what happened when they were growing up, and when they start a relationship with a woman, they think she will be just like their mother.

Let's face it, if you work all day and come home to a clean house, the kids are bathed and ready for bed and your dinner is on the table, who wouldn't want that?

I don't want to be a man basher and say that ALL men don't contribute to raising a family, but when it comes to looking after the household chores and the children, we all know that the large percentage of men need to do more.

The 2016 Australian Census[23] showed that women spend up to 14 hours a week on housework while a man does fewer than five

---

[23] https://www.abs.gov.au/websitedbs/censushome.nsf/home/2016

hours a week; therefore, women still do most of the household chores even when they work full-time, just like the men.

Trying to break old habits is not always an easy thing to do. One thing I realised I was doing was appeasing men. When I got married, I used to iron my husband's shirts. Then one day I thought, *Why the hell am I doing this when I have my own clothes to iron for work?* I quit doing that, but I still did most of the cooking. My husband was like most men who were raised in the '60s and '70s and did not do household chores, that was what his sisters did. It was the same when I grew up; my brother never helped with the housework, it was up to my sister and I to clean up the house when we got home from school.

After reading a book by Louise Hay called *Empowering Women*, I realised that the generation I was raised in made most women subservient to men. It has been that way for too long.

Even when it came to the jobs I had, I also appeased men by not saying anything when inappropriate comments were made. I just kept quiet and let it slide. The sayings 'men will be men' and 'boys will be boys' come to mind. Women need to stop being silent, but I know that's easier said than done when it comes to keeping your job or even avoiding an argument with your partner or husband and ensuring your safety.

They say that in time things will change and that much has changed already. But why should women wait? We have waited long enough.

We have all heard the statistics when it comes to equal wages between men and women, and I have had discussions with men about this topic. Men are adamant that women get the same wages as men in equal positions. I never did, and I have known other women in the same position. In government jobs they usually do, but the private sector is a completely different story.

The comment has also been said that women have a lower wage because they don't do the same jobs as a man.

The Australian Bureau of Statistics state that women comprise 77.9 percent of those working in health care and social assistance, and men make up 87.3 percent of those working in the construction industry. The average wage of, let's say, a nurse is $73,000. The average wage of a man in construction is $111,000.[24] Both of these jobs require a degree (average is four years) so you have to ask:

Why does a construction worker deserve to get paid more than a nurse?

Unfortunately, in our capitalist society a construction worker is valued more than a nurse. It seems totally ridiculous that this is the case because our health is way more important than constructing a building. If everyone in the world got sick and nobody could work, you wouldn't have people constructing buildings. It should be health before wealth. If we have health, then wealth will follow. Or redefine the value of wealth as being good health! After all, what else is more valuable?

Profit before people is the unsaid motto when it comes to most large corporations, and yet many don't even pay taxes. At the G7 summit of world leaders in 2021, there were efforts to force

---

[24] https://www.abs.gov.au/statistics/people/people-and-communities/gender-indicators-australia/nov-2019

multinational companies to pay a fairer share of tax.[25] This was after 130 countries and jurisdictions agreed in June 2021 to plans for a global minimum corporate tax rate.

The principle of the agreement is that multinationals would be forced to pay a minimum of 15% tax in each country they operate in. It also includes plans to prevent the shifting of profits into tax havens by tech giants and other multinationals by enabling signatory countries to tax the world's largest companies based on revenues generated within their borders.

Many companies also save money when it comes to women's wages. *Estimates for average weekly ordinary time earnings for full-time adults (seasonally adjusted):*

- *Males: $1,970.90 (public), and $1,770.30 (private).*
- *Females: $1,762.00 (public), and $1,475.50 (private).[26]*

When you look at these figures of full-time average wages, even in the public sector women get paid less, but it would be because it's mostly men in the senior positions.

In the most recent ABS statistics, retirees with no personal income stayed around 30 percent for women and 7 percent for

---

[25] https://www.bbc.com/news/world-57368247
[26] https://www.abs.gov.au/statistics/labour/earnings-and-work-hours/average-weekly-earnings-australia/nov-2020

men.[27][28] Women suffer greatly at an older age financially due to taking time off to have children, plus getting paid less than men.

The increasing numbers of older women in Australia are experiencing, or are at risk of homelessness, with a rise of over 30 percent in just five years.[29] Experts recognise that due to the 'hidden' nature of older women's homelessness, these figures may not represent the full extent of the issue today. There is a range of underlying structural and cultural factors leading to women's economic disadvantage. This, coupled with an ageing population, means that the risk of homelessness among single older women is projected to increase.

I completely understand why a lot of women stay in marriages even when they are unhappy, as it is difficult to set yourself up financially if you leave. Staying in a relationship keeps a roof over your head. I was only able to keep a roof over my head and have financial independence because I moved to the country and purchased a house at a much lower price than purchasing one in the city.

Now that I am a woman in her fifties, I am past my child-bearing years, not married and currently in the fastest-growing group of people that are homeless. In only the last five years the number

[27] https://www.abs.gov.au/statistics/labour/employment-and-unemployment/retirement-and-retirement-intentions-australia/latest-release#:~:text=to%202%25).-,Income%20at%20retirement,of%20income%20for%20most%20retirees.&text=Retirees%20with%20no%20personal%20income,women%20and%207%25%20for%20men.

[28] https://humanrights.gov.au/our-work/gender-gap-retirement-savings

[29] https://www.aihw.gov.au/reports/homelessness-services/specialist-homelessness-services-annual-report/contents/unmet-demand-for-specialist-homelessness-services

of middle-aged women either homeless or couch-surfing has doubled.

Yes, *doubled*. How sad is that.

Many women find themselves in controlling and abusive relationships. If they try to leave, they face the threat of violence or even death. The rise in deaths of women who leave partners continues to increase, perhaps because more women are standing up and finding the courage to leave but their partners are far from happy about it and they seek revenge.

Over the past decade the number of women who have been killed by their partners, husbands and men in general has increased so much that it is at crisis levels, but sadly the perpetrators often seem to get off lightly. In our male-dominated world, it seems that a woman's murder or rape is often not seen as that important. Governments say they are going to do more, but it often seems to be just lip service.

Key findings from the Australian Government Department of Health and Welfare for Homelessness Services[30] are:

> *In 2019–20, on average, there were 260 unassisted requests per day; a total of 95,300 unassisted requests for 2019–20, which was 3,000 more than in 2018–19 (92,300).*

> *Three in 5 (60%) unassisted requests involved short-term or emergency accommodation and over 1 in 4 (26%)*

---

[30] https://www.aihw.gov.au/reports/australias-welfare/homelessness-and-homelessness-services

When l left my husband, I had to go on unemployment benefits as I was not working at the time. It wasn't something I wanted to do but something I had to do. I tried to get work but jobs for women over fifty were thin on the ground. Some jobs I didn't get because I was overqualified, I mean, what the hell is that all about! Other places clearly just wanted someone younger.

So many women are discriminated against in the workplace due to having time off to have children. Then when you are older and your child-bearing years are well and truly over, you are seen as too old! Seems like we can't win either way.

Why did it take the COVID-19 pandemic for women to be seen? 2020/21 were interesting years to say the least, but with all the bad things that happened, some interesting things came to the surface about women in society.

Women continued to be more adversely affected by the labour market deterioration than men. Data gathered by ABS showed the percentage of men and women in various industries saw women taking the brunt of job losses in the retail and accommodation industries.[31] While we saw shops and the hotel industry crippled during the pandemic and mainly women being impacted, we also saw that it was mostly women who were at the front line in healthcare and education. The construction and building industries had only minimal stoppages but when they were closed down for a couple of weeks due to not abiding by regulations on building sites many construction workers held violent protests. If they followed COVID regulations on site the industry would not have shut down.

The industries with the highest proportions of women and men have remained consistent over the past decade.

In 2019–20, the industries with the highest proportion of women aged 20 to 74 were:[32]

- *Health care and social assistance (77.9%)*
- *Education and training (71.6%)*
- *Retail trade (55.2%)*
- *Accommodation and food services (54.5%)*
- *Administrative and support services (52.9%)*

In 2019–20, the industries with the highest proportion of men aged 20 to 74 were:

- *Construction (87.3%)*
- *Mining (83.0%)*

---

[31] https://www.abc.net.au/news/2020-05-06/fears-coronavirus-will-destroy-financial-independence-for-women/12217672
[32] https://www.abs.gov.au/statistics/people/people-and-communities/gender-indicators-australia/latest-release#:~:text=In%202019%E2%80%9320%2C%20the%20industries,Retail%20trade%20(55.2%25)

- *Transport, postal and warehousing (79.8%)*
- *Electricity, gas, water and waste services (76.2%)*
- *Manufacturing (72.5%)*

In a world dominated by men in the political and corporate arenas, it has become glaringly obvious that women were our saviours during the pandemic. As much as we need the industries that men dominate, when it comes to our basic survival, that is where the women rule. I see them as the givers in the world, and when it comes to takers, I think most people will agree they are politicians and large corporations. Corporates are only concerned about their own profits and that is where greed comes into play.

So much has changed around how we work now due to COVID-19. Many people started working from home as they couldn't go into the office. Working from home, if you are able, is so beneficial to families and, in particular, it has given working mums more flexibility to juggle family life plus earn a living and have a career. This is something most families have been wanting for a long time but few companies have provided it.

The structure of going into the office and working 9–5 while management hovers around making sure everyone is working is how it has been for so long. I have worked in many places where talking was frowned upon, and God forbid if you laughed. It was all work and no play, and I can assure you these were horrible places to work and they usually had a high staff turnover. Poor management try to whip people to work to 'get their pound of flesh', but it doesn't make people work harder, it just makes them more resentful.

In the lead up to completing my first draft of this book so much happened when it came to women rising up and wanting to be heard. First, Grace Tame's voice gave other women the courage to speak up about abuse. One of these was Brittany Higgins. Approximately four weeks after Brittany came forward, information regarding allegations of an historical rape by Christian Porter were forwarded to various politicians.

The allegations against Christian Porter were damning and there was a push for an inquiry, but Prime Minister Scott Morrison considered the matter closed due to the woman in question dropping the rape charges two days before she allegedly committed suicide. Due to the Prime Minister refusing to have an inquiry, the women of Australia were outraged and within ten days a March4Justice[33] protest was organised, and women from all around Australia were encouraged to take part.

It wasn't just about the abuse of women, which sadly there are many, but March4Justice was calling on the public to sign a petition addressed to Scott Morrison, which made a series of concrete requests to put an end to the issues of sexism, misogyny, patriarchy, corruption, dangerous workplace cultures and lack of equality in politics and the community.

A protest was organised for 15th March 2021, in Treasury Gardens near Parliament House in Melbourne, and I was naturally drawn to this protest. It was scheduled for midday and I arrived around 11.15am. Many women had already arrived, and all were dressed in black, as requested by the organisers. Approval was given for this protest to occur (not an easy thing when COVID-19 restrictions were still in force). They estimated

---

[33] https://www.march4justice.org.au/

that about 1,000 women would attend. COVID-19 restrictions were enforced with mask wearing and social distancing.

I watched as thousands of women (and some men) walk down the paths toward the podium that was a small truck parked in the middle of the gardens. It was a powerful sight watching these women in black walk in with their placards. It showed to me that women are bloody sick and tired of being treated like second-class citizens and not being heard. They are sick of having their issues swept under the carpet by white privileged men who dominate not only our governments but also most of our large corporations and businesses, in Australia and around the world.

It is amazing to think that this happened because of one Tweet in late February 2021, by Janine Hendry asking women to join her to protest at Parliament House in Canberra because she was angry about how Scott Morrison was handling sexual allegations within his own party.

Volunteer leaders around Australia created events in more than 200 towns and cities. Some 110,000 women and their allies stood up, spoke up and were heard around the world.

A strong message was sent to our government.

Sadly, on the very day of this march, Christian Porter filed a defamation lawsuit against the ABC and reporter Louise Milligan who published the story on his alleged rape of a woman back in 1988.[34]

---

[34] https://www.abc.net.au/news/2021-05-06/christian-porter-applies-strike-out-parts-abc-defence-defamation/100122360

On 19th September 2021, Christian Porter resigned from parliament as it was discovered he accepted money to cover his legal fees in a defamation case with the ABC, and that he accepted money from an anonymous donation from a 'blind trust', which is against parliament protocol. Christian Porter and the government of Australia did everything in its power to stop this story from getting out.

At the rally I listened to the women on the podium speak passionately about their experiences. I knew then and there that I had to complete my book and let others know my story, even though I was petrified about letting family and friends know the truth about not just the sexual harassment and discrimination that occurred, but how I'd spiralled into the black hole and almost took my own life.

I recall being petrified about going to court when I was discriminated against, but I pushed forward and eventually won my case. It wasn't easy, and the same can be said for all women standing up for equality – it will not be easy, and history has proven that. Women have had to fight for their rights, and we will have to continue that fight for many years to come. It saddens me greatly that women have to do this, but while we live in a world that is dominated by men in powerful positions, real change will not happen until more women are in positions where they have the power to change how this world is today.

Equality, it is not just for women but for everyone, and that includes all denominations, colours, sexual orientation, gender, young and old. I do believe that when we have more diversity in positions of influence, the current patriarchy system will be destroyed.

Women around the world need to stand up, be brave, have their voices heard and to stop being silent. I was silent about the sexual harassment that occurred to me in the workplace and thought, *Boys will be boys*. Well, not anymore. Men have to stand up and be accountable for their behaviour, and we all need to work together and make the changes that are desperately needed to make this world a better place for everyone.

It has been extremely daunting for me to write this book, but I know in my heart that with determination, women around the world can make a difference and in some small way I hope I am too.

Both men and women need to come together and forge a path for more compassion and sympathy because what is going on now is simply not working.

I know there are lots of good people out there trying to make this crazy world a better place and that many stand up and make themselves heard and to get the message out that the way society is today and how we move into the future has to shift dramatically. With our patriarchal society and most mainstream media being controlled by rich white men it can be difficult to get your message out.

As a woman I want to get my message out that a lot has to change in the world when it comes to how we treat one another. I don't want to cry anymore, I want to live a happy and safe life, laugh with my friends and family and simply enjoy life in a world where we have more kindness, respect and love. Sounds cheesy? Yes, it does in a way but that is what I would like, and I know many others feel the same way.

Chapter 24

My life now

When I started to write this book, I had no idea what I would call it. Some things came to mind like, My Jobs Made Me Mental, Corporate Craziness, Fucked Up at 50, Work Is Making Us Crazy. But learning more about myself I realised I am a strong woman, but I have also been great at covering up my sadness.

That's when I came up with *Strong Women Cry Too*.

I look back and see how much my life has changed and I am happy to say for the better. I never thought in a million years when I got married at the age of twenty-two that in my fifties I would be single, living in a seaside town away from the concrete jungle doing meditation, yoga and painting to try to keep my life on track.

For one, I never thought I would actually complete a book.

As my life changed and through all that I experienced, I felt more and more drawn to tell my story about how hard life can be for women. I don't want to say that men don't have difficulties, but they most certainly don't have to deal with many of the challenges that women have to deal with.

I have been writing for over seven years now. I originally wrote to get shit out of my head as it helped. I had written so much, and I had a lot of material to work with and then I was finally encouraged to just do it, and by a man. This also showed me that some men do see how women struggle in a male-dominated world and that when we work together it can only be a good thing.

I hope that writing this book will help others with depression and anxiety so they can recognise that hiding it is not going to make it go away. I also hope that more women will come forward and speak out when it comes to being discriminated against, not just in the workplace but also in society in general.

When it comes to our workplace laws, particularly when it comes to women having a baby, these laws should have more protection for women to return to work after having a child. Our government would say that we have laws to protect women but as I have discovered these laws have been watered down over the past twenty-five years and it is much easier to dismiss any employee under the current redundancy laws that I have mentioned early in this book.

Looking back, I know that my personality may have contributed to the way people treated me. Having spoken to some people I worked with, they most definitely said that I spoke up if I saw something wasn't working well in a workplace. It may have been an office procedure or how a customer was being neglected. My heart was always in the right place, and I just wanted to ensure that customers were given the service they were paying for. I know that some managers didn't like this but others I worked with appreciated my honesty and they would look at making things better for the sake of the business.

Our lives have become so busy and our minds need to catch up sometimes. Taking time out to just have a short rest is the best thing you can do if you've been running around like a maniac. Interesting to think that the increase in wild, angry, violent and destructive behaviour has increased rapidly in the past twenty years. I believe it's because we are becoming maniacs, *busy, busy, busy*, no time to even breathe.

It can be hard work trying to keep, not just our general health in good condition but even harder for our mental health. Having a mental health condition is just like any illness you are the only one that can make yourself better. You can take medication, exercise, do meditation, in fact do anything that makes you feel better. The mind is such a powerful thing, and we don't really take into account how much it controls our body and thoughts.

It's great to try to keep fit. I love to do yoga and swimming, but I've also learnt that meditation is very important as it slows the mind down. The brain needs to have a rest, not just in sleep but a conscious slowing down. I find that if I haven't done meditation for a few days then I do feel wound up. Many people think meditation is all about 'Ommm-ing', but *it's not*. They think it's some type of hippy thing. You don't have to sit cross-legged on the floor with incense burning. You can sit or lie wherever you want. You might even do it in the car, not while driving, of course, but you may have just parked your car at the shopping centre.

When people used to speak about being spiritual, I had no idea what it meant. I just thought it was another religious thing, but now I know it's not.

I didn't really think I was spiritual until I realised that a lot of the things I was doing were, in fact, spiritual. When I finally googled what being spiritual was, I found twelve signs that you are spiritual:

1.	You gaze at the stars.

2.	You try to think happy thoughts.

3.	You offer a helping hand.

4.	You feel serenity in nature.

5.	You follow your guided intuition.

6.	You seek the truth in all situations.

7.	You honour life.

8.	You're appreciative of the smallest bug to the largest animal.

9.	You recognise the power of forgiveness.

10.	You strive to detach from drama.

11.	Travel is appealing.

12.	You have a heart of humour.

From a young age, I looked up at the stars and wondered what else was out there. I have always believed in UFOs as I simply don't believe we're the only planet in the universe that has life. How can you look up at all those stars and not think that something else is out there? On those nights when the sky is clear and you can see the Milky Way, I love to sit back and just gaze up. It's so beautiful and peaceful as well.

When it comes to happy thoughts, I did, for a long time, think I was happy when in fact I wasn't. It was only when I realised how unhappy I was, that I started to question life. I thought, this can't possibly be how my life is going to be. It was the time when I left my husband and then finally moved to the beach. It still took me a couple of years to finally be happy and grateful for what I'd done to change my life and the courage it took to get to the place where I am now. If you are truly unhappy in life, it is not easy to change, but it can be done. If you want to live life and be happy and fulfilled, it is up to you to change it. Nobody will do it for you.

I still look back and see how much my life has changed. It does take time to forgive and forget (though you never forget people who have really hurt you) and move forward. Forgiving someone is a process but, more importantly, forgiveness is for you, so you can let go of the bad thoughts and look to the future and not the past.

I have always felt that I offered help when someone needed it. I am a good listener and I had lots of people who could talk to me easily. Sometimes, though, you must be careful that these people are not sucking the life out of you. You need to draw a line in the sand as to how much you will help someone. If you feel you are giving too much of yourself, then you *must* pull back.

I have always loved nature and don't understand people who don't. Some people love the concrete jungle and the fast lane, but not me.

As for seeking the truth in all situations I believe that we all want the truth even if it hurts. In society today the truth on many things that are happening around the world are covered up, not just by our political leaders but also many large corporations who benefit from hiding the truth.

When I finally moved away from the city to the beach, I finally felt more peaceful. The longer I've been here, the more enjoy it. When I go to bed at night and can hear the waves, I just love it. In the morning when I hear the birds singing and playing in the gutter of my house where water pools, it brings a smile to my face. Sitting on the beach just taking in the sounds of the wind, the water and the smells is one of the best things you can do.

As I've grown older and, hopefully, wiser, I've realised that life is short and the years fly by. I've learnt to do the things I love and love the people who treat me right. I do what makes me happy and be content with life. I try not to worry about what other people think but I think that is a challenge for most people.

I have one chance at life, so I don't want to waste it on things that don't really matter.

In mid-2019 I made the decision to come off anti-depressants, and by early 2020 I had managed to get off them completely. It was a long process, and you should never come off them quickly as you need to monitor how you are going without them. This is also done in consultation with your doctor.

When I finally came off them completely it was an awful experience, with constant chills, headaches, dizziness, agitation and brain zaps. Brain zaps feel like an electric shock to your head, and I absolutely hated them. Doctors tell you that anti-depressants aren't addictive, but as far as I'm concerned, they most certainly are. The longer you've been on them the harder it is to stop taking them. It probably took three to four months before my brain zaps stopped, and I almost went back on anti-depressants because of them.

I managed to stay off anti-depressants for about ten months when I realised I really did need something to help with my anxiety. I still got depressed but not as much as I used to, and with the help of meditation, yoga, painting and walking on the beach, I kept it at bay. It didn't help that the COVID-19 pandemic was impacting the world, which made many people depressed for the first time in their lives. I'm glad I had these techniques before the pandemic hit.

I started to look around for a more natural way of dealing with my depression and anxiety, and I finally looked into medicinal cannabis. Unfortunately, it's expensive to purchase, and you also have to fit the requirements for a doctor to administer it. The main one is that you have to have tried other prescription medications before you're allowed to use medicinal cannabis. As I fit this requirement, I made the decision to give it a try.

I have written in the book that I used to smoke marijuana, and I admit that I first smoked it when I was young at parties. In later years with everything that happened in my life, I started to smoke on a more regular basis because it chilled me out and made me less tense. I know the whole smoking thing is really bad for your health, but I liked the fact it made me calmer. When I did smoke marijuana, I felt great shame about it. A lot of people close to me knew I smoked, and I knew a lot of people who did the same. They're not people who sit around a coffee table and pull bongs all day. Most of these people have professional jobs and good standing in the community. I wasn't the only person hiding a secret of taking illegal drugs.

I gave up smoking, both cigarettes and cannabis, completely about four years ago now and don't miss it at all. When I read the medicinal cannabis research and how it's proving to be effective in many illnesses and also mental health conditions, I made the decision to give it a go.[35]

The benefits I have found to using this drug instead of anti-depressants is that I don't have to take it every day. You have to take anti-depressants every day, and if you don't you feel wiped out. I always knew when I'd forgotten to take my medication as I would wake up dizzy and in a total brain fog. Once I took a tablet it would probably take about half a day before I felt okay.

With medicinal cannabis, I don't have an issue at all if I don't take it, and when I feel my anxiety and depression (more so my anxiety now), I take some. I don't feel like I'm chained to it and that if I get to a stage where I don't need to take medicinal cannabis anymore, I know it will not take me more than six months to get off it.

So, you have to think, *What is more addictive?*

For many years I wanted to give up marijuana as I hated keeping the secret that I still smoked it. I find it funny how I've come full-circle and can now take medicinal cannabis prescribed by a doctor to help my condition.

Sure, I have times when my anxiety increases but, on the whole, I'm healthier than I have been in a long time. I try to do yoga twice a week, walk somewhere every second day and ride my bike. I don't overdo it but moving is definitely better for the

---

[35] https://adf.org.au/insights/medical-cannabis-mental-illness/

mind. I continue to paint and might have the same canvas going for many months until I complete it. I think painting is a great form of meditation as it takes you to a different place and stops you from constantly having shit spinning around in your head. The picture on the front cover of this book is painted by me. I call it *Bright colours beneath the sadness*.

I still have to deal with my tinnitus, which is sometimes a bit maddening, but if I'm not stressed then the buzzing isn't as loud. I do believe it started because of stress and also the fact I was in flight or fight mode so much that I used to clench my jaw, and this caused temporomandibular joint dysfunction (TMJ). The medicinal cannabis also helps with the pain I get from my jaw.

When I ended up in hospital, I had been involved in a local theatre group, helping out with props. It was a wonderful distraction where I learnt lots of artistic skills and met some wonderful people. Only a select few knew that I had been hospitalised, and that is how I wanted it to be. I made good friends with a woman who had many challenges in her life, and we bonded while making a massive sixteen-foot dragon for the production of *Miss Saigon*. It was a massive task, but rewarding, and the head of the dragon still hangs from the ceiling at the shed where all the props are made. To this day I consider this woman a dear friend.

It was due to my involvement in the theatre group that I decided to take up painting. I was really awful at first, but painting became a form of therapy and eventually I was asked to do paintings for friends. There is an increasing amount of scientific evidence that proves art enhances brain function. It impacts brainwave patterns and emotions, the nervous system, and can actually raise serotonin levels. Art can change a person's outlook and the way they experience the world.

I called my paintings my mental health projects. I joke when I say that to other people but painting definitely helps your mental health.

I get back to Melbourne and see my son and family members as much as I can but in recent times, with COVID-19, that has been difficult, but no different to anyone else who is experiencing the lockdowns.

So many new people have come into my life, and I get out and about more than I did twenty years ago. I still love to cook and it gives me great pleasure to have someone over for dinner.

I help out with a dear friend's holiday rental place, and I still see her on a regular basis. We have some wonderful chats about life and the things that have happened to us. It's better for us than going to a psychologist. I have also reconnected with a friend from my youth who moved to the area. She too has had many challenges in life, although I was reluctant to reconnect with her at first because she was still in contact with people from my past, and I felt protective of my new life. I soon realised we were able to talk about the past and she knew most of my story. She also helped me mourn the loss of old friends and be grateful for what I have achieved in my life. She could see that I had great strength in moving away from Melbourne and starting a new life.

I do some dog minding too. The extra money is most certainly welcome when you live on a pension. I still feel guilty about the fact I'm on a pension, and I have tried to find work in the area, but it scares the shit out of me. If I find myself in a horrible workplace again, I am terrified of falling back into the black hole. I have absolutely no trust in any workplace and have little trust in managers doing the right thing by me. I know some are out there, but they are hard to find.

I'd like to be more involved in helping organisations see that they need to clean up their act. If they do, the benefits for the people who work for them will be immeasurable, both financially and emotionally. Also, our youth need to be taught at an early age how to deal with the struggles that occur in life. They need to know life is not all about living it through your mobile phone and that nobody's life is perfect. Our world is spinning out of control, and although many people are raising awareness of mental health issues our society is still largely consumed with wealth, power and greed.

We need more places where we can go and get away from technology, truly take in the fresh air and talk to others about our struggles and know that we are not alone. A place where we can heal and get ourselves ready to move forward in the next phase of our life because you know it's going to change. Being admitted to a psychiatric ward is not the answer for many mental health conditions, in fact, for me it was the worst environment I could have been placed in. Prevision is much better than the cure.

At the start of 2020 I felt like I was finally getting my life on track, then COVID came along to knock me over, but I was lucky to be living by the beach and able to breathe the fresh air. I was unable to see my son, but we kept in contact as much as we could. I was glad he was still able to work. If I'd been working when COVID-19 came along I probably would have lost my job yet again.

As 2020 rolled on, I was encouraged to continue to write, not only by my phycologist but also by my friend Alex, whom I first met on a yoga retreat at Magnetic Island. He said my story needed to be heard. If it helps anyone and makes them understand they're not alone then that makes me feel good about myself as well.

It has scared me to write this book, but we need to be brave and strong, tell our story, as that is when we will see more change.

Patriarchy will not save the world. We all need to be kinder to one another and the planet for humanity to survive. I hope that I will see change in my lifetime and that in some small way I hope I have helped.

So, whatever small thing you might do to help improve our world, go and bloody do it, even if it scares the shit out of you. I can assure you that letting everyone know my story and putting it in the public arena scares the shit out of me.

Be brave, be strong, move forward with your heart and know that things can change if we all do our bit to make that happen.

References

- https://www.fwc.gov.au/documents/documents/benchbookresources/unfairdismissals/unfair-dismissals-benchbook.pdf
- https://www.legislation.gov.au/Details/C2021C00189
- https://humanrights.gov.au/our-work/sex-discrimination/publications/respectwork-sexual-harassment-national-inquiry-report-2020#fn1
- https://www.theguardian.com/culture/2021/jun/21/sony-music-australia-allegations-toxic-work-culture
- https://humanrights.gov.au/our-work/sex-discrimination/publications/respectwork-sexual-harassment-national-inquiry-report-2020
- https://www.gfmag.com/global-data/economic-data/largest-companies
- https://www.afr.com/politics/federal/anthony-albanese-imposes-labor-bonk-ban-20201111-p56dls
- https://www.abc.net.au/4corners/inside-the-canberra-bubble/12864676
- https://www.who.int/news-room/fact-sheets/detail/suicide
- www.aph.gov.au
- https://humanrights.gov.au/our-work/education/womens-rights
- https://www.gs-press.com.au/wp-content/uploads/sites/21/old_upload_files/1997/Jordon%20v%20Amcor%20Ltd%202%20May%2097.pdf
- http://www.austlii.edu.au
- https://www.fairwork.gov.au/employee-entitlements/types-of-employees/casual-part-time-and-full-time/casual-employees

- https://www.aph.gov.au/About_Parliament/Parliamentary_Departments/Parliamentary_Library/pubs/rp/rp1718/CasualEmployeesAustralia
- https://www.abc.net.au/news/2020-11-12/rachelle-miller-michaelia-cash-office-complaint/12873818
- https://humanrights.gov.au/sites/default/files/2020-10/AHRC_AR_2019-20_Complaint_Stats_FINAL.pdf
- https://www.pc.gov.au/__data/assets/pdf_file/0019/249040/sub629-mental-health.pdf
- https://www.pc.gov.au/inquiries/completed/mental-health/report
- https://www.smh.com.au/politics/federal/parliament-has-a-drinking-problem-so-it-s-time-to-consider-a-booze-ban-20210331-p57fhv.html
- https://finalreport.rcvmhs.vic.gov.au/recommendations/
- https://www.pc.gov.au/inquiries/completed/mental-health/report/mental-health-actions-findings.pdf
- https://www.mayo.edu/research/centers-programs/center-regenerative-medicine/focus-areas/liver-regeneration
- https://www.abs.gov.au/statistics/people/people-and-communities/gender-indicators-australia/latest-release
- https://www.police.vic.gov.au/100-years-women-policing
- https://www.abs.gov.au/statistics/labour/earnings-and-work-hours/average-weekly-earnings-australia/latest-release
- https://humanrights.gov.au/our-work/gender-gap-retirement-savings
- https://www.news.com.au/national/politics/scott-morrison-apologises-for-wrong-remarks-about-news-corp-harassment/news-story/ab0fefeeaa8ab36fed99806684c3cfe9

- https://humanrights.gov.au/our-work/age-discrimination/publications/whats-age-got-do-it-2021
- https://www.abs.gov.au/statistics/people/people-and-communities/gender-indicators-australia/nov-2019
- https://www.abc.net.au/news/2021-06-24/barnaby-joyce-to-sit-on-cabinet-taskforce-for-women/100242078
- https://www.ourwatch.org.au
- https://www.abc.net.au/news/2020-01-28/how-police-are-failing-survivors-of-sexual-assault/11871364?nw=0
- https://www.oprah.com/inspiration/what-oprah-knows-for-sure-about-mental-illness
- https://www.theguardian.com/business/2021/jul/01/global-tax-reform-130-countries-commit-to-minimum-corporate-rate
- https://www.police.vic.gov.au/100-years-women-policing
- https://www.abc.net.au/news/2021-07-15/parliamentary-sexual-harassment-workplace-training-optional/100293784
- https://iview.abc.net.au/show/ms-represented-with-annabel-crabb
- https://humanrights.gov.au/our-work/gender-gap-retirement-savings
- https://www.abs.gov.au/statistics/labour/employment-and-unemployment/retirement-and-retirement-intentions-australia/latest-release
- https://www.aihw.gov.au/reports/homelessness-services/specialist-homelessness-services-annual-report/contents/unmet-demand-for-specialist-homelessness-services
- https://www.lifeline.org.au/resources/data-and-statistics/
- https://www.healing-power-of-art.org

- https://www.medicalnewstoday.com/articles/how-long-after-stopping-antidepressants-before-i-feel-normal-again#symptoms-and-timelines
- https://adf.org.au/insights/medical-cannabis-mental-illness/
- https://carnegieendowment.org/publications/interactive/protest-tracker